THROTTLING THE RAILROADS

OTHER BOOKS BY
CLARENCE B. CARSON

The Fateful Turn

The American Tradition

The Flight from Reality

The War on the Poor

THROTTLING THE RAILROADS

Clarence B. Carson

Published by

LIBERTY FUND, INC., INDIANAPOLIS, INDIANA

for distribution by

THE FOUNDATION FOR ECONOMIC EDUCATION, INC.
IRVINGTON-ON-HUDSON, NEW YORK 10533 1971

CLARENCE B. CARSON, is Chairman, Social Science Department, Okaloosa-Walton College. A native of Alabama and a graduate of Auburn University, he holds the Ph.D. from Vanderbilt University. His field of specialization is American social and intellectual history. He is a lecturer of note in his chosen field, the author of several books, and a frequent contributor to various scholarly journals.

THE FOUNDATION FOR ECONOMIC EDUCATION is an educational champion of private ownership, the free market, the profit and loss system, and limited government. It is nonprofit and nonpolitical. Sample copies of the Foundation's monthly journal, THE FREEMAN, as well as a list of books and other publications, are available on request.

Published May, 1971

Printed in U.S.A.

Contents

Preface

THIS LITTLE volume belongs, loosely, to a cycle of works which took shape as a result of my writing *The Flight from Reality,* which was published as a book by The Foundation for Economic Education in 1969 but which had been published serially in *The Freeman* during a 26-month period from 1964 into 1966. To that point, most of my writings could have been classified as social and intellectual history, though they had somewhat of an economic focus to them as well. Since writing *The Flight from Reality,* my work has gone decidedly over into economic history. What I was trying to say in that book thrust me in this new direction.

The idea I was working with in *The Flight from Reality* was that the reformist and interventionist ideas and practices which have been gaining headway over the last eighty or ninety years have not produced the results which presumably motivated and have frequently been claimed for them. On the contrary, the results have frequently been the opposite of what they should have been, according to the claims. I tried to show that the reason for this lay in contradictions between the reformers' notions of it and reality itself.

As for the results, however, I alluded to them only in *The Flight from Reality*. After that, it became important to spell them out. One reason that this led me to economic history was that the reformers had focused so much of their attention on economic matters. Another was that the cause and effect relationships involved seemed to me more clearly traceable in the economic realm than, say, in the moral realm or in literature, for instance. That may have been so because I had become increasingly sensitized to the economic realm. In any case, the cycle of works to which I referred at the beginning has dealt most extensively with economic history.

The first work after *The Flight* was *The War on the Poor* (New Rochelle: Arlington House, 1969). The theme of this book was that government programs that were supposed to help the poor have usually harmed them. This was followed by "The Rise and Fall of England," published serially in *The Freeman* (1968-1969). As is probably obvious from the title, this was a broad-scoped work dealing with several hundred years of English history. One of its main themes was that government intervention in the economy of England contributed greatly to the fall of that country from its former leading role in the world.

The present work attempts to trace the effects of intervention on a particular industry—that of the American railroad industry. The pattern of the cycle of works goes from the general to the particular. If it were carried one step further, the effects of intervention on a particular company might be examined. Many academicians trained in the English-speaking world may suppose that I have gone about the matter wrong-end-to, that I should have gone from the particular to the general rather than from the general to the particular. The inductive method is frequently described as involving the latter order of working and presenting findings.

I could object that that is not the way I worked, that I worked from the general to the particular and that is that. But that would be to make an unnecessary confession of personal eccentricity which, in this case, would not be correct. In point of fact, the general rule is that the acquisition of knowledge proceeds from the general to the particular, that is, proceeds from certain premises, theories, axioms, or principles. This is as true of what is today referred to as scientific knowledge as of any other kind. We did not make exploratory flights into space after which we concluded that the universe is governed by laws uniform in their operation. On the contrary, this premise was implicit in the Copernican system, and was explicit in the work of Kepler and Newton. True, we have had some amazing empirical confirmations of the validity of this premise in recent years, but the odds against our having acquired the information by making the flights without the premise of uniformity are too great to guess at. In the same manner, scientists did not go from the particulars of atom smashing to the formula $E=MC^2$. It was the other way around. They did not even discover the atom before smashing it; instead, they posited such a unit and theorized about it.

It is said that water cannot rise above its source. It can be said with equal validity that our knowledge cannot expand beyond our theoretical framework. The reason for this is simple enough; we would not know what we knew if we knew something outside a framework for knowing it, which is a way of saying that we could not know such a thing. All this is by way of saying that our knowledge is an unfolding of what is implicit in our premises, theories, and principles. This makes the premises and their correctness most important. I have long thought so, and have taken care from time to time to set forth some of those on which I was working. They are testable, too, but since philosophy has fallen into its present disuse many premises go untested. Both reason and evidential particulars play a role in this testing.

This cycle of works, then, has followed the norm by moving from the general to the particular. The railroads turned out to be a happy choice for an industry in which to examine the impact of intervention. They have been subject to intervention for a long while in American history. Everyone admits that the railroads are in some sort of crisis. This little book attempts to show how this state of affairs came about. It does so tracing the story of the building of the railroads, their operation and development over the years, and the intertwining of intervention with these. The framework for this tale is the nature of railroading, the nature of government, the nature of man, and the nature of economy. These premises would enable us to project that the outcome of the intervention would be what it has, indeed, been.

Something else led me to a particular study of the railroads. I have long been fascinated by trains, by their operations, their history, their terminals, and their schedules. My interest has never been quite so active as to qualify me as a railroad buff. But it has been sufficiently extensive to prompt me eventually to have the temerity to write something about them.

I have been most fortunate in my writing over the years to have done so much of it for The Foundation for Economic Education and to have had a good bit of it published in the Foundation's journal, *The Freeman,* in which most of the chapters first appeared. A writer's work is, by its nature, lonely. So much of writing is done in solitaire, laboriously struggling in the silence to fill the paper void before one with words. Once the words have been shaped into something larger—an essay, an article, a chapter, or whatever—most writers then have a great urge to exhibit, one which I share. We would run into the street to grab the first passerby and present him with a reading of the fruits of our labor. Unfortunately, strangers rarely tolerate us, and our list of friends grows shorter on each presentation. We learn, after awhile, to restrain our exuberance, to send our work off to an editor, and to await his verdict, realizing that, however long it takes to hear from him, it will take much longer before it is finally published and a more general verdict is in. I like to write books, even, but the length of the task overwhelms me.

A part of my good fortune in having done much of my work for The Foundation for Economic Education is that much of this waiting has been foreshortened by them. Dr. Paul L. Poirot, the editor of *The Freeman,* is dependably prompt and decisive in dealing with work submitted to him. I have even been enabled to write what turned out to be books, a chapter at a time, have the chapters published serially, and get some results long before a book would be published.

My gratitude to The Foundation, and to Leonard E. Read who directs its course and informs its actions with his vitality and integrity, has deeper dimensions than the above. Most of my work goes against the grain of the spirit of the times. The worshipers of the state and the apologists of intervention have held sway in the academy and most of the publishing world since I can remember being aware of such things. FEE has made it possible for me to have my say; it has been worth much to me to be able to do so, though of the value of my work for others I can hardly be the judge.

My thanks go to Mrs. Eleanor B. Orsini who has done the work of reading and correcting copy quietly and efficiently. Of course, none of the people who helped me with my work should be blamed for any errors of fact or invalidities of interpretation which may appear in this book. The responsibility for any of those is unavoidably mine.

My wife, Myrtice Sears Carson, has not only put up with the inconveniences of having me spend so much time at writing but also has aided me materially by reading copy before it went off to the printer, listened to my disorganized notions about how I proposed to proceed on the work, and applied herself diligently to providing peaceful surroundings in which I could work.

CLARENCE B. CARSON
Ft. Walton Beach, Florida
February 20, 1971

1 Prologue: A Nostalgic Look at the Passenger Train

IN MY LIFETIME—which from my angle of vision hardly seems to have been very long—I have traveled in most of the ways man has devised. I have traveled on foot, by which I mean "traveled" to get from one place to another, not just an after-dinner stroll to aid my digestion or defer heart ailments. When I was a boy on the farm, travel on foot was my most common means of locomotion. My experience with this means of transport was broadened during World War II and for a while afterward by a hitch in the United States Army. Walking may be good for the health, getting underway is simplicity itself, capital expenditures are minimal, but it is no way to go sightseeing. Vistas, even charming ones, tend to pall long before they pass from view, and things come into view so gradually that the element of surprise is wanting.

I have traveled on horseback. To my way of thinking, however, it is generally overrated. It contains too many elements of uncertainty to make for relaxed sightseeing or for predictable movement from one point to another. Horses are temperamental beasts, skittish and given to sudden alterations in their pace. If the horse is at all tall, one is an alarming distance from the ground which has a definite penchant for leaping up at one as the horse comes down and retreating even further away as the horse gallops along. Moreover, to my knowledge no more uncomfortable mode of traveling has ever been conceived than riding a horse. Rumor has it that there are gaits which are as smooth as can be, but none of the animals I have ever mounted was practiced in them: they all jog in such a way as to threaten the continuity of the backbone and disturb the peristaltic action of the innards.

I have traveled, too, in various conveyances drawn by animals. The least elegant of these was undoubtedly the farm wagon with metal-rimmed wheels. Not only was the pace apt to be little more than it would be for a man afoot but also the uncomfort index was usually high. Even a springed seat could do little to cushion the impact of the wheel on pavement or rough unpaved road, as the case might be. Buggies, as I remember them, were usually drawn much faster than a wagon and might have the luxury of padded seats, but few people mourned their passing.

I have, of course, traveled in a considerable array of internal-combustion-engine driven vehicles. Probably my first ride was in a Model "T"; first and last, I rode in an assortment of those, mostly of the open-air variety. There is no denying the adventure of setting out on a journey in one of these; anything or nothing might happen, for there was no great certainty that it would even crank, but there were several means by which that condition might be achieved. However, the Model "T" was already giving way to more dependable, comfortable, and less adventurous automobiles when I can first remember such things. There were makes of cars over the years that are no longer in production: Whippets, Nashes, Studebakers, Hudsons, Packards (whether I ever rode in a Packard or not I cannot now remember, but it was an elegant automobile), and so on, as well as the numerous models of makes still available. In addition to cars, I have ridden in jeeps, trucks, buses, and a motor home. On one occasion, I even took a spin around the corner on a motorcycle, with someone else steering it, but my inclination toward comfort and safety has led me to spurn this primitive conveyance.

There is no denying the excitement as one sets out on a journey by automobile in the early morning, nor of the convenience of starting out from one's home and going all the way to the destination in one's own vehicle, nor the satisfaction of being the driver of a powerful machine, nor of the determination of one's own course. There are some drawbacks, however, to automobile travel: notably, fatigue, danger, cost, and the fact that the driver must do much of his sightseeing in glances stolen from the highway.

I have traveled by airplane, too, though not by any other airborne contrivance. Undoubtedly, the jet plane is the most expeditious way in commercial use to get from one point to another. Air travel is exciting—occasioned in part by apprehension, in my case—the stewardesses are usually attractive, all things connected with it have a bustling atmosphere which suggests that here is where the action is, and the service is usually good. There is no getting around the fact that traveling by whatever means can be wearying and, on occasion, tiresome. Fast airplanes get the trip over quickly, thus reducing the fatigue factor in travel. They boost the ego, too, in a fairly subtle way, for speed suggests that one's time is very valuable. Of course, there is no substitute for an airplane in an emergency when someone needs to travel a considerable distance.

But the airplane has numerous drawbacks. As far as "travel" in the sense of sightseeing, a change of pace, and relaxation, the jet plane traveling at a speed of 600 miles per hour at an altitude of between 30-40,000 feet has almost nothing to offer. The ground below is usually a hazy blur in daylight frequently obscured by clouds, and at night a black void relieved occasionally by the lights of cities which are, undoubtedly, a spectacular scene sometimes. An intermediate trip is over too quickly for relaxation; the stewardesses scurry about to try to get the meal served, and if one dawdles over a drink or coffee he may miss the meal. If the trip is longer so as to cross several time zones, the disturbance of the daily rhythm interferes with the normal alternation of activity and rest.

Sightseeing in Comfort

All this is by way of leading up to the point that so far as travel over land is concerned only one means of travel has yet been devised which affords ample opportunity for relaxation, comfort, rest, sightseeing, time for adjustment to different time zones and changes in altitude or climate. That is travel by passenger train. Compared with all other surface or air travel, the passenger train can offer more extensive accommodations, greater luxury, and more comfort. For sightseeing in comfort with a sense of well-being, nothing can compare with sitting in a diner, being served a fine meal by highly skilled waiters after having been seated by a steward, gazing out at the scenery for which the train travels fast enough for surprises yet slow enough to take in all the vistas. Not all trains nor all of the accommodations are equally luxurious, but, at the worst, crowded coaches that may be old enough to be classed as antiques offer opportunities to look out, to walk about, and seats wide enough for comfort.

My own travels by train have been quite extensive, though I have never traveled for the purpose or with the intent of writing about it. Therefore, I have no notes or other aids to the memory to rely upon. Even so, they do include the use of most of the kinds of railroad facilities that have been available in the last thirty or forty years.

My first trip by train contained all the elements which would make such travel pleasurable, save one: it was not voluntary. I had just been inducted into the United States Army and was about to begin extensive travels at times and to places most of which were not of my choosing. It was in June of 1944. The trip by train got underway from Atlanta, Georgia. It had one element in it which most such trips do not have but which heightened interest and apprehension. For some reason, or unreason, those of us in the detachment did not know our destination, nor did any amount of pleading succeed in prying the information from the officer in charge. If the others felt as I did, it would have been all right for the trip to last on and on, for when it was over basic training would be our common lot.

We boarded the train at what must have been Atlanta's Union Station (the smaller of the two main stations there) around dusk of a June evening. I had no basis of comparison at the time, but I can say now that our accommodations were spacious and luxurious. There must have been just enough of us in the detachment to occupy one Pullman sleeping car. This was not an old open section sleeping car, nor one of those used on troop trains. It was an all room car, and the room in which I traveled must have been either a compartment or a drawing room.

The train left the station around dark, and by the towns through which we passed I could know we were headed in a southwesterly direction. I can now reconstruct the route that we took. We left Atlanta on the rails of the Atlanta and West Point Railroad, thence on the Western Railway of Alabama from West Point, Georgia, and in Montgomery joined the iron of the Louisville and Nashville which took us to New Orleans. We passed through Mobile in the first light of day and reached New Orleans early in the morning. There was a twelve- or fourteen-hour lay-over in the Crescent City.

Ordinarily, people speak of "lay-overs" in much the same fashion as they do of lengths of stay in a hospital. But this one was not like that. We were in no hurry to get to our destination. We walked about the streets of the city, had lunch in a deliciously cooled cafeteria, and then took a trip down the Mississippi in a multi-decked sightseeing boat. Meanwhile, our Pullman had been transferred to another station and another train. We left New Orleans on a Southern Pacific train sometime after dark.

Next morning, the train was moving down the track somewhere in east Texas. This was fabled country to a boy grown up in the Southeast and nurtured on Saturday Westerns. By midafternoon, the train had pulled into the station at San Antonio. I remember looking out from air-conditioned comfort at the sweltering heat, the workmen icing the cars from great blocks of ice sitting on a cart, and, if memory serves, at the palm trees around and about the station. By now speculation was rife as to our destination. Could we be going to California? The prospect gladdened, not only because it was yet a long way off but also because for a lad who had never been more than a hundred and fifty miles or so from home before, it would be quite a distinction to go there.

More of Texas passed us by while light remained that day. One gets a sense of the length of that state when it is noted that we were still in Texas the next morning, though the train had been moving consistently on its way. California was not our destination; we reached that all too quickly when the train pulled into El Paso, Texas, and we were suddenly, as it were, standing outside in the scorching heat waiting for a truck to take us to Fort Bliss. The Sunset Route of the Southern Pacific stretched on toward California from there, but our journey was ended.

The Long Way Home

I was by no means finished with train travel, of course, nor, for that matter, train travel in Texas. When my basic training was finished, I was transferred to Camp Carson, Colorado, which is just outside Colorado Springs and was given a furlough—a delay en route, it was called—of fifteen days. It is somewhat out of the way to go from El Paso, Texas, to Colorado Springs by way of Alabama, but that is what I did, for understandable reasons. The Texas and Pacific had two trains east at that time. One left in the morning, the other probably late in the afternoon. The one that left in the afternoon was a through train which would speed me on my way to Memphis. The one that left in the morning was a nondescript train whose destination was Fort Worth. There was no doubt which was the better train for me—the afternoon train—but I did not take it. My leave began in the morning, and I was determined to be on my way, though I would reach my destination no sooner by doing so. My accommodations were not luxurious this time. I was paying my way, so I settled, of necessity, for coach travel. The steam locomotive pulled this train across the plains of Texas at a snail's pace, or so it seemed to me, for I was eager to get home this time.

Railroad buffs of the steam engine may have forgotten some of the niceties of travel on some trains pulled by them. The engineer started the train one car at a time, giving a tug and a jerk which was followed by the bump into the car ahead. The wheels were not really flat on this train, but they clacked and clattered mightily against the rail. If I remember rightly, during the day and night of travel we experienced the range of temperatures available. It was commonly said that there were only two temperatures on a passenger train, too hot and too cold. On some, this was very nearly true. Yet, such a trip had many elements common to most train travel: the wait after boarding until departure, the slow starts, the long thrusts through the countryside, the stops at out-of-the-way stations, and so on. The demographic shape of Texas becomes apparent on this trip: the hundreds of miles of wasteland in the West and then towns of increasing size and number as Forth Worth and Dallas get nearer.

A lay-over through a long day brought the through train into the station toward late afternoon. From Fort Worth to Memphis the journey was by way of the Texas and Pacific which somewhere along the way almost insensibly becomes the Missouri Pacific. From Memphis to Birmingham the train was over the St. Louis and San Francisco—the "Frisco"—a railroad which does indeed go to St. Louis but never got anywhere in the vicinity of San Francisco. This might have been the *Kansas City-Florida Special;* if so, it was a fancier train than I had been on of late. The Frisco goes through towns with such interesting names as Holly Springs and Tupelo in Mississippi and Winfield in Alabama.

The last leg of my journey was on a mixed train on the Atlanta, Birmingham and Coast Railroad—which was later sold to the Atlantic Coast Line, which is now the Seaboard Coast Line—which ran from Birmingham to Manchester, Georgia. A "mixed" train is one which has a consist of freight and passenger cars. The freight cars rode ahead on this one, and two passenger cars followed at the rear. The train stopped at places to pick up passengers where no station was to be seen. But I reached home by way of it, and that part of the journey was not long.

My trip back followed about the same route to Fort Worth, except that there was a wreck somewhere in Texas on the Texas and Pacific which led to a re-routing of the train I was on by way of the St. Louis-Southwestern Railroad. On this trip, I noted a difference between the steam locomotives used in the Southwest from those in the Southeast. They used oil to fire the boiler. That undoubtedly made the fireman's job less taxing, for the oil was fed into the flames by lines while coal had to be scooped into the fire by hand in the East. From Fort Worth, I traveled northward on the Fort Worth and Denver and then the Colorado Southern to Colorado Springs. This took me through Amarillo on a cold late autumn afternoon; it looked truly forbidding, windswept, and uninviting.

I had, by this time, seen a great deal of Texas by rail, from Beaumont and Texarkana in the east to San Antonio, Dallas, and Fort Worth in the center, to El Paso in the west, to Amarillo in the Panhandle. Texas is a vast state, having within its bounds most of the extremes of climate, varieties of produce, and seasonal changes which could be named. The trip which took me through Amarillo, Texas also took me into the Rocky Mountains, and I saw for the first time the huge steam engines with their bulging boilers made necessary by the grades the trains must negotiate.

Streamliner to St. Louis

My stay in Colorado was brief. Two things happened almost simultaneously to make it so. My outfit was ordered to Oklahoma, but before the move I got an emergency leave to return home to Alabama for a few days. The train out of Colorado Springs was the Missouri Pacific's *Colorado Eagle,* if I have remembered correctly, and it was my first trip on a streamliner. I caught the train at night; by morning we were on the plains of Kansas. The train brought me to St. Louis sometime around midday. The station at St. Louis must be one of the most wondrous railroad sights in the world. There may be larger waiting rooms or places on which more trains have converged, but none that I have seen has such a panorama of tracks to look at all at once, as it were. If my memory is right, I counted fifty tracks all on the same level, occupied by dozens of trains in various stages of readiness for departure. Here, passenger traffic from virtually every point in America converged on a single depot. When the passenger train was the way to travel, this was one of a few major focal points where East met West to join the United States.

I boarded an undistinguished Louisville and Nashville train later on in the afternoon, a train which would take me to Birmingham by morning. But first, it had to travel to Evansville, Indiana, and, to my way of thinking, this route through southern Illinois into southern Indiana goes through some of the most beautiful pastoral scenery in America. As I remember it, there were steep hills and green valleys on which sheep and cattle were grazing. Much of it is rolling country, and there can be few scenes more pleasant to the eye as one rolls through the countryside by train.

Train schedules were none too dependable during that wartime. This fact was brought home to me this time as I made my way back to camp, this time to Camp Gruber, Oklahoma. There had been a wreck on the Atlanta, Birmingham, and Coast, if I have the time right, and I had to travel a ways by bus to catch a Central of Georgia train into Birmingham. The Frisco train was pulling out there when I boarded it. This was largely an illusion, however, for it proceeded only a short distance before it stopped, to stand for what must have been a couple of hours on a siding. No amount of highballing toward Memphis succeeded in making up for lost time. I missed my connection at Memphis; thus, I waited for about 23 hours to catch a streamliner on the Chicago, Rock Island and Pacific, a train which must have been called the *Rock Island Rocket.* This train took me within a few hours to McAlester, Oklahoma, where, in the middle of the night, I caught a mixed train of the Missouri-Kansas-Texas—the "Katy"—which took me to Muscogee.

There may be no ready way to get from Camp Gruber, Oklahoma to Fort Meade, Maryland by rail. If there is, the Army did not find the route when it dispatched us on this journey. We boarded a Missouri Pacific train pulled by a huge steam engine late on a winter's afternoon. The train headed in a southeasterly direction, to Fort Smith, Arkansas, thence to Little Rock, then on to Memphis, which we reached by early morning. There, we changed to a Southern Railway train, but we were not finished with going south to get north. It took us all of the daylight hours to get from Memphis to Chattanooga, but most of the trip was not through Tennessee. The Southern route descends into Mississippi at Corinth, then proceeds across Mississippi through northern Alabama before it finally turns northward in east Alabama to go to Chattanooga. This must have been a name train, for it had Pullmans and there was an observation platform on the last car. It was exciting to stand on it and to be in the open air as the train moved by indirection toward a distant goal.

By the next morning, we were somewhere in Virginia; sometime during the night we had switched from the iron of the Southern to that of the Norfolk and Western and would shortly switch back to the Southern, if we had not already done so. Sometime during the day we approached Washington, D.C., and could see before we got there the glistening Capitol off in the distance, as fine a sight as there is in the world. From Washington northward we were in the domain of the Pennsylvania and the Baltimore and Ohio, several of whose trains I rode in the next couple of weeks.

Along the Busy Tracks of the Pennsylvania

My last stop before going overseas was at Camp Kilmer, New Jersey. This camp is within an hour of New York by a slow local train and is located next to the main line of the Pennsylvania. We had little to do during the few days we were there; the weather was cold and snowy most of the time, and I spent much time inside during the days. The window from the barracks faced toward the main line of the Pennsylvania. The time was early in the year of 1945. War production was at its height. Much of the produce of America was flowing overseas to Europe, and it left from the eastern ports of the United States, above all, from New York City.

This must have been the busiest section of a railroad in the whole world; certainly, it was the busiest line I have ever seen. There are four through tracks, two for traffic in each direction, one for slower and one for faster trains. It was almost impossible to look out and not see a train headed one way or the other; more often, there were two or more in view. The characteristic Tuscan red of the Pennsylvania predominated in colors of freight and passenger trains, but almost every sort of freight and passenger car might be seen. Much of the rail traffic of America converged on these lines. From the many points of the South it funneled into Washington by way of the Richmond, Fredericksburg and Potomac and the Southern, then much of it on to the North by way of the Baltimore and Ohio and Pennsylvania. From the great cities of the Midwest it came, from St. Louis, Chicago, Cincinnati, Indianapolis, and Pittsburgh, and from the metropolitan areas of the East, from Baltimore, Philadelphia, and lesser cities. Much of this traffic, in turn, had been gathered from more distant points in the West and Southwest at the rail centers to which the Pennsylvania ran. The mind boggles at imagining how that continuous stream of traffic could have been handled at terminal points in New Jersey and New York City. Yet handled, it undoubtedly was.

Trains were very much a part of my life for the next several weeks, but ships were, too. We went by train to the port of embarkation. We disembarked from the ship at Liverpool, England, only to board a train once more. The English trains were miniatures compared to those in the United States, their cars smaller, their engines much smaller, and even their whistles more like a child's shrill sound than the throaty blast of an American steam locomotive. Even so, they moved with great dispatch from city to city through the English countryside.

The sun was shining brightly as the train glided out of Liverpool, making the red brick houses, as alike as peas in a pod joined to one another in a continuous manner broken only by the intervention of streets, appear redder than they could have been. The train followed a route from the northeast to the southwestern city of Southampton during the course of the day. It passed through countryside much of which was green even in midwinter and all of which was neatly laid out in plots so well kept that the patterns were pleasing to the eye from a train window in the way that American farm country is only when seen from the air. There was only one bad moment during a day of rewarding sightseeing. While we were stopped in a station—I think it might have been in Birmingham—I saw a British soldier with a rifle on his back. This reminded me that I was not just out to see the sights but on a mission to places where men deal in death and destruction. For a moment I panicked, but it was only for a moment; life and the will to experience are too strong in a nineteen-year-old to be contained by thoughts of death.

Trains of Europe—in Wartime

After an all too brief stay in Southampton, we boarded ship for a night crossing of the English Channel to Le Havre, France, a city that was not so much fronted by a harbor at this time as an extensive wreckage from bombings. After only the briefest of respites at what passed for a camp on the outskirts of this city, we boarded a train in the late afternoon of the next day. This was the least elegant of trains imaginable; it was a passenger train only because it carried passengers. In point of fact, it was a freight train with a consist of cars which have been known since World War I as "forty and eights." That is, the train was made up of European-sized box cars to each of which could be assigned eight horses or forty men. I believe eight horses would have been much more comfortable than forty men were. The box cars had no accommodations except bare floors and walls. The trick was to find sufficient room to lie down on the floor without smothering someone else or being smothered. Thus we traveled for a span of about twenty-four hours, northward through France and into Belgium. Of France I remember little, for most of our journey through that country was accomplished at night.

Belgium seemed to be made up of a continual stream of industrial cities, unrelieved by any significant amount of intervening countryside. One picture still comes vividly to my mind as I recall the latter part of that trip. It is of the large number of steam locomotives standing on sidings out of action. The boilers of most of them were riddled with holes made by machine gun bullets. A steam locomotive with a head of steam is as alive as an inanimate object can be, steam pouring from every opening, their insides gurgling from boiling water, panting to be underway. These great engines with the back part of their boilers flared into great bulges were lifeless, standing like so many wounded elephants unable to fall because their legs were locked in the joints, mute victims of a war that had now retreated to other terrain.

My experiences with trains, for the time being, came to an abrupt end at some city in Belgium whose name I no longer can recall. After the war in Europe was over, I rode a good many trains on the continent, but there was only one trip worth recounting. In April of 1946 I finally got to go on a Swiss-Rome Tour, as it was called, a trip I had been wanting to make for some time.

Those of us going on the tour boarded the train at Munich, Germany. Early the next morning, we were at the border of Switzerland. This would have been apparent even if we had not had to go through customs, for Switzerland was another world from the war-torn Europe I had known for more than a year. Switzerland is a land of spectacular mountains, valleys, and lakes. Surely, no way of seeing it can quite compare with the view from the window of one of its electrically motived trains.

The train takes you through cuts in the snow and ice of glaciers, beside towering mountains, through tunnels from which you burst of a sudden upon a beautiful lake surrounded by snow-capped mountains as a background. If the spirit is not up to the appreciation of such beauty continuously, the train comes to its aid by arriving at a city. Swiss towns and cities look as if they had been washed down and polished before breakfast. The streets are neat, the streetcars gleam, and the shops have the appearance of being reconstructions such as are sometimes made in America by foundations. Italy was, by comparison, a more pedestrian sight, though no Swiss city can match the history-laden spectacle of the Eternal City, Rome.

The Great Period of the Passenger Train

The decade after World War II was in some ways a great period of the passenger train. Passenger miles traveled declined, of course, from the gasoline-scarcity war years. The steam locomotive was giving way almost completely to the diesel engine. The airplane was already beginning to lure long distance travelers away from the railroads. Even so, many railroads spent great sums on streamlined trains with domed cars and enclosed solariums on rear end cars. Streamlining had begun in the late 1930's. The practice grew of having whole trains constructed of stainless steel and appearing to constitute a single unit. These, in turn, were frequently painted in the bright colors of the livery of a particular line. Pullman Standard cars were relegated to undistinguished trains. The streamliners could be things of beauty, indeed. The blues of the Baltimore and Ohio and Louisville and Nashville were distinctive, as were the yellow stripe on blue of the Chesapeake and Ohio. The Tuscan red trains of the Pennsylvania were so numerous that one frequently failed to note how outstanding they could be. The Atlantic Coast Line's varnish trains sported purple trim, the Southern Pacific's reddish orange, yellow, and black, the Northern Pacific's a bright green, while other lines stayed with the silver finish on stainless steel.

American passenger trains could be divided, roughly, into four categories. Heading the list would be a very select number of premier trains. These trains were usually all sleeping cars, at least at their inception, were noted for their food and service, made the best time between points of any train on the line, had dome cars if they passed through scenic country, and had the finest equipment on a major railroad. Among these select trains—each in its heyday—would be included the New York Central's *Twentieth Century,* the Pennsylvania's *Broadway Limited,* the Seaboard Coast Line's *Florida Special,* the Illinois Central's *Panama Limited,* the Burlington's (and connections) *California Zephyr,* the Santa Fe's *Super Chief,* the Great Northern's *Empire Builder,* the Northern Pacific's *North Coast Limited,* the Southern Pacific's *Sunset Limited,* the Baltimore and Ohio's *Capitol Limited,* the Rock Island-Southern Pacific's *Golden State,* and Union Pacific's *City of Los Angeles.*

The most magnificent train I have ridden was the *Super Chief.* The first time I rode it from Chicago to California was in June of the mid-1960's. It was an all Pullman train on that trip, followed by a section containing at least some Pullman's, followed on the same schedule by the coach hi-level *El Capitan.* Everything about the train was elegant, the service in its beautiful diner, the lounge with the starlight dome car above it, and the rooms which were equipped with music selected to the taste of the occupant. There is spectacle enough on this trip: the morning passage through Raton Pass, the sight of the gleaming *Chief* meeting on the way, the multicolored Rocky Mountains of New Mexico heightened by a fading afternoon sun, breakfast just before arrival looking out at the superb wastelands of California. I have ridden the *Golden State,* too, a portion of the trip along the Sunset route beyond El Paso which was denied me on my first train trip. When I rode it, the consist of cars was not nearly so impressive as those of the *Super Chief.* It had maintained, however, a reputation of long standing for excellent meals and, what impressed me much, there was a finger bowl for each diner.

Near Champs, and Also Rans

Some of the second category of trains would be only slightly less impressive than the premier ones; indeed, some of them were once of the first rank. After World War II, they were all streamliners and were known by their names. Here there were so many that only a few names on the roster could be called. They would include the Pennsylvania's *Spirit of St. Louis,* the Pennsylvania-Louisville and Nashville's *South Wind,* the Illinois Central's *City of Miami,* the Southern's *Southerner* and *Royal Palm,* the Atlantic Coast Line's *West Coast Champion,* the Seaboard's *Silver Meteor,* such Burlington trains as the *Denver Zephyr,* the *Texas Zephyr,* the Santa Fe's *San Francisco Chief* and *Texas Chief,* among many, many others.

Below these were trains which had names quite often but were fitted out with indiscriminate equipment, which had fallen on evil days from earlier prime. At the bottom of the list would be trains usually having only numbers, occasionally having a mixed consist of freight and passenger cars, operating on very slow schedules, and stopping at numerous places to deliver mail and an assortment of parcels.

There are trains that I have not ridden that I would like to ride, to see sights not seen or from a different perspective. The Pacific Northwest has been a major omission in the United States. It would be good to see it from the windows of either the *North Coast Limited* or the *City of Portland*. The Milwaukee-Union Pacific's *City of Los Angeles* runs through country I would like to see. To change coasts, I would like to ride over the Great Smokies on what was, or is, the Southern's train from Knoxville to Asheville, to rise against the grain of the French Broad River as that incomparable mountain stream ripples and splashes on its leisurely way into Tennessee.

But I count myself fortunate to have been able to see so much of America through the windows of train cars. I have seen, on several occasions, the skyline of New York City looming ahead as trains approached the city, have seen the endless rails and almost numberless factories of Chicago spread out before me, have followed the course of the Mississippi River northward toward St. Paul on a Burlington *Zephyr* on a wintry day and seen the broad expanse of the Mississippi with its surface sufficiently frozen that cars could stand on it, have glided through the Southern Delta by train, have seen the waters of the rivers at Pittsburgh by night illumined by the glow from the furnaces, have crossed the Alleghenies on a day when a deep snow was falling on the *Pennsylvania Limited,* have crossed the Alleghenies when they were spectacular in summer foliage on the *Capitol Limited,* have gone down the marshy east coast on the Seaboard's *Silver Comet,* have seen the plains of Texas and the plateaus building toward the Rockies. These trains have terminated at some of the world's great train stations: Pennsylvania Station, Grand Central, Union Station in Chicago, and the magnificent station at Cincinnati.

He who has ridden the rails has, whether he knew it or not, been a part of and felt the sinews of America. The pounding of steel wheel on steel rail has for long now been the commercial and fraternal heartbeat of the United States. For more than a century, produce has flowed from the hinterland of America to the cities where it was wanted. From these same cities have gone forth goods to the most remote hamlet which brought the conveniences of city life to the countryside. Wheat from the Great Plains, iron ore from Minnesota, steel from Pittsburgh, clothing from New York, citrus fruit from California, Texas, and Florida, cotton from the Deep South, vegetables from states with mild winter climates, automobiles from Detroit, and thousands of other products from this land of diverse climate, topography, and fertility have flowed by way of the rails to those who would buy them. We have now devised means of communication which do not require wires for messages to be sent and received. Other systems of transportation have been devised to supplement or supplant the railroads. Yet none of these is likely to equal the railroad as a means for experiencing the expanse of this country as a United States. For that, the passenger train has been without peer.

2 The Railroad Problem

AYN RAND put her finger adeptly on the jugular vein when she focused attention on the railroads in her novel about the economic breakdown in the United States, *Atlas Shrugged*. Surely, the colossus of the Western Hemisphere, the United States, rose to eminence in the world on the gridwork of steel rails that spanned its length and breadth and reached out like fingers to touch the farthest corners of a vast half-continent. Before the coming of the railroads, to speak of a *United* States was to speak in the hyperbole of politicians and dreamers. These United States were separated by great chains of mountains, by formidable bodies of waters, by natural obstacles which carved the country into regions, sections, isolated valleys, and vast well-nigh untappable hinterlands. Railroad builders sought out the mountain passes, followed the cuts made by streams through the ages, bridged the rivers, and laid the rails across the stretches of flatland. They united the states commercially, politically, and, mayhap, fraternally.

Indeed, the American railroad system is one of the marvels of the modern era. There were 23 miles of track within the United States in 1830; by 1920 there were 252,845 miles. Most of the trackage was laid between 1870 and 1910, in one of the most propulsive construction programs ever undertaken in history. By the early twentieth century, virtually every town and hamlet in the country was either on or within a few miles of a railroad, and most towns of any size had service by two or more railroads. Cities were frequently served by a half-dozen or more companies, two or more of these frequently connecting with the same distant points. Peoples and goods moved over these lines with speed and safety which a few generations before could hardly have been conceived.

In a recent advertisement, the Association of American Railroads attempted to evoke a sense of the marvelous character of this means of transportation. It read, in part:

> Suppose that everybody in the United States were to learn for the first time about a marvelous method of transportation called a railroad.
>
> The idea would be sensational.
>
> High-speed tractors running on steel rails laid on privately-owned rights-of-way, with minimum curves and grades, would be capable of pulling long processions of trailers full of merchandise. Imagine!
>
> Trains of trailers would be kept rolling day in and day out until they reached their destinations. They would be shuttled into and out of marshalling yards, where the trailers would be grouped in the right combinations. Of all things! . . .
>
> The high-speed tractors on their twin ribbons of steel could even haul human beings, in addition to freight. If necessary, the human being could be bedded down and hauled from one place to another in special cars with comfortable seats and all the comforts of home.[1]

A Waning Romance

Americans have not always been oblivious to the marvels of the railroads, of course. On the contrary, many have long been fascinated with this way of transporting people and goods. A good case could be made that many Americans have had a long romance with the rails. The story of the railroads is deeply entangled in American lore, legend, and history: the buffalo hunters, the clashes with the Indians, the rush of the railroad crews to lay rails into the West, the driving of the golden spike at Promontory Point to celebrate the linking of the Union Pacific and Central Pacific, the bigger-than-life gangs of train robbers—epitomized by the James boys—, the ballads such as "Casey Jones" and "Wabash Cannon Ball." The steam engine was itself a thing for wonder and awe: steam spouting from its sides as it stood in the station, its lonely whistle in the night, the huffing and puffing as it made a long grade, its long sigh to let off steam as it came to a halt. Even the mighty diesels, while

---

[1] Quoted in John F. Stover, *American Railroads* (Chicago: University of Chicago Press, 1961), p. 248.

not so romantic as the steam engines (probably because they are still with us), could cause heads to turn and voices perforce to cease or be unnaturally raised as they roared by.

The railroads capitalized on this interest and tried to build excitement by the names they gave to their crack passenger trains in the twentieth century, names which suggest that the trains soar, ramble, move swiftly, and fly as they rush to make their destination against the clock, names such as *Twentieth Century Limited, Silver Star, California Zephyr, Spirit of St. Louis, City of Los Angeles, South Wind, Sunset Limited, Empire Builder, Super Chief,* and *Rocky Mountain Rocket.* Even some freight trains have been given special names; the Milwaukee Road calls a westbound fast freight the *XL Special* and its eastbound counterpart the *Thunderhawk.*

Even so, the railroad advertisement is probably right in what it implies: the American people are no longer generally enamored of the railroads. They have spurned many of the rail services with alacrity and taken much of their custom elsewhere. Even the mention of railroads evokes a faint nostalgia in response. The impression grows that they are obsolete, that their ribbons of steel stretching off into the distance are becoming mute monuments to days gone by, their passenger stations relics of other times, their forms about to be reduced finally to toys in the basement and Sunday rides on narrow gauge lines to old abandoned mines. At any rate, the railroads are in trouble. As one writer puts it: "There can be no doubt about the severity of the railroad problem facing the nation in the sixties."[2] The railroads have had a long-term trend of declining traffic, both passenger and freight, though the decline in freight has sometimes been only in the proportion of total freight hauled. Service has been increasingly curtailed. Railroad stocks have long failed to respond even to proportionally higher dividend-to-cost ratio than most other stocks. These are the almost invariable signs of a dying industry.

Still Essential for Transport

Yet, the railroads remain an essential method of transport in America. Not only were they once crucial to the commercial unity of America; they still are. It is true these United States are now linked together by

---

[2] *Ibid.*, p. 47.

Union Pacific Railroad Museum Collection

The meeting of Central Pacific and Union Pacific locomotives at Promontory Point, Utah, May 10, 1869.

highways over which gasoline engines pull trucks and automobiles, that these highways, presently being supplemented by an interstate system, reach more places than the railroads, and that any city of any size has many which form junctions within its borders. But these vehicles which travel on the highways are an increasing source of trouble themselves. They pollute the air; they converge on the cities at certain hours of the day constricting movement and raising tempers; parking places for them become ever more costly and difficult to find. Trucks increase in number and size on the highways, vying with automobiles for travel space and increasing the peril of travel. The carnage on the highways is so great that anyone sensitive to the propaganda about it must set out even on a vacation trip in an automobile with considerable apprehension.

If that portion of the freight now carried on trains should suddenly be shifted to the highways, the pace of traffic would be drastically slowed and much that now moves that way could hardly find a place. We are already experiencing the impact on highways of the shift of passenger traffic from trains to private cars, for the most part; what it would be like when freight should be as preponderantly shifted to the highways as are the passengers can only be left to the imagination. As things stand, many cities probably could not survive such a shift; many of them are already marginal as places to live, and transport is one of the major reasons. This is why the railroads remain an essential method of transport for America. Yet, the long-term trend in a shift away from them is now well established.

Deterioration in Quantity and Quality of Service

Why should this be? To the casual observer or unwitting customer it often appears that the railroads are their own worst enemies, that the management and personnel are directly to blame. Those who use the railroads frequently get the impression that the roads are determined to be rid of them. This is most noticeably the case with passengers, but users of freight service of certain kinds may get a similar impression. Anyone who has ridden the trains often in the last decade or so probably has his own list of complaints. The list will most likely include such items as reluctant ticket sellers, difficulties in acquiring information, late departures of trains, late arrivals, surly employees, inconvenient schedules, dilapidated equipment, long walks to cars past a line of cars for mail and parcels, lackluster surroundings from beginning to end of journey, and so on.

Stories abound of horrendous treatment of passengers by the railroads. The present writer has seen a restroom in a passenger station to which entry could be gained only by dropping a coin in a slot, has heard a porter utter such streams of profanity about the difficulty of getting a woman's luggage from one train to another that she offered to carry it herself to shut him up, has had his rest disturbed by noisy "deadhead" railroad employees on several occasions, and has seen any number of waiting rooms sufficiently gloomy to discourage all but the most intrepid traveler by rail.

Some of these might be only individual instances of poor service which can happen in any undertaking. But there is much testimony that they are of a kind that occurs all too frequently on the railroads. One writer notes that "except for a few crack transcontinental and other trains, the quality of service rendered has deteriorated compared with prewar [World War II] years. . . . Trains are frequently late; coach equipment is often old and sometimes dirty and poorly ventilated and heated. Many prewar standards of courtesy have gone, even in parlor and sleeping cars. . . . On some of the best coach routes, the railroads use obsolete passenger train cars and treat customers as though the carriers were doing travelers a favor to transport them."[3] Another says, "The public sees the railroads as old fashioned . . . , and as common carriers who hate passengers."[4]

Suicidal Practices

It certainly looks as if the railroads were trying to commit suicide. They have low advertising budgets compared with other businesses; the uniforms of their personnel appear to date back to the beginnings; their passenger stations frequently appear to be a combination of late Victorian grandeur gone squalid and early government housing projects; their freight stations are often a poor imitation of a down-at-the-heels hardware store. The following are instances of how railroads have alienated passengers:

> Take, for example, the process of calling on the telephone for some scrap of information about a passenger train. . . . Some railroad clerks are evidently instructed to take their phone from its cradle, or hook, and then to forget it. . . . Other railroad clerks, themselves impervious to minor irritations, simply ignore a ringing phone, hour after hour. . . .
>
> Another stratagem is the disruption of train schedules. . . . Suppose you wish to travel overnight by train from Washington to Memphis. There is no through service, but the Southern Railway has a Birmingham Special that arrives in Chattanooga at 8:10 A.M. or ten minutes *after* the train to Memphis has left. The Southern Pacific's Sunset Limited has been so rescheduled that, eastbound, it no longer connects at New Orleans with the Gulf Wind . . . , westbound, the Sunset leaves stranded in New Orleans for about fifteen hours those passengers coming from the east on the L and N's Crescent or the Southern Railway Southerner.[5]

[3] James C. Nelson, *Railroad Transportation and Public Policy* (Washington: The Brookings Institution, 1959), p. 321.

[4] Stover, *op. cit.*, p. 251.

[5] Peter Lyon, *To Hell in a Day Coach* (Philadelphia: Lippincott, 1968), pp. 267-68.

While freight traffic is not so cavalierly treated, many small communities have lost their agents, and many kinds of package freight do not appear to be much wanted.

Not all railroads have been so disdainful even to their passenger customers. But even those who have continued to serve long distance and commuter passengers well, often say that they are losing money. Lately, a considerable movement has been mounted for governments to subsidize passenger trains, and some of this is already being done.

A Puzzling Performance

There are two enigmas here. In the first place, it is not usual for businesses to discourage customers and treat them as if they were not wanted. Private enterprise succeeds by serving customers and by gaining and keeping their good will. Even losses may be sustained to provide certain kinds of service in order to gain profitable custom. When businesses behave otherwise, this behavior requires explanation. The second enigma is why any good or service that is widely needed and wanted cannot be profitably provided. Commuter trains, for example, may be filled to overflowing during rush hours, but many railroads no longer wish to operate them. Transportation is not the only area where the provision of vital goods and services has sometimes become unprofitable (others would include food provided by farmers and rental housing), but it is certainly a crucial one today. This is, to say the least, enigmatic.

There is, of course, an explanation. To get at it, it is necessary to look into the history of the railroads. Even the most casual student of American history will recall certain facts related to railroad history. Even the most general history of the United States will probably mention land grants to railroads, the Railway Strike of 1877, the Interstate Commerce Act, the Pullman Strike, the Northern Securities Case, the government take-over of the railroads in World War I, and the Transportation Act of 1920. In short, what the casual student may discern with a little reflection is that there is a long history of government involvement with and intervention in the affairs of the railroads. Deeper examination will show the impact of this on the railroads and provide explanations for the strange situations that have developed.

There are three fundamental reasons, then, why anyone undertaking to write an anti-utopian novel about the United States, as Ayn Rand did, might well focus on the railroads; and they are reasons why a historical study of the railroads is warranted. First, the railroads were crucial in providing a means for commercially uniting the states, and are a still vital part of the transportation network of this country. Second, they have been in trouble for a considerable while and have suffered a long-term decline. This has brought in its wake a host of other problems already alluded to. And third, there is a long history of government intervention in rail transport with all its ramifying effects.

Indeed, the railroads are the classic example in American history of the impact of government intervention on a business. They have had the longest history of intervention by the Federal government of any modern business. Theirs was one of the earliest instances of extensive subsidies to more or less private undertakings. The first strike to have an impact on a goodly portion of the country was against the railroads—the Railway Strike of 1877. The first general act to regulate interstate commerce and the first national regulatory commission was aimed at the railroads—the Interstate Commerce Act and the Interstate Commerce Commission. One of the earliest applications of the Sherman Antitrust Act by the Supreme Court against a portion of an industry was made against the railroads in the Northern Securities Case. The railroads were the first private industry to be taken over and run by the Federal government for a time—during and after World War I. In short, except for banking and the delivery of the mails, the railroads have probably the longest history of intervention of any major business in the United States. Nor is there any better place to study the debilitating effects of this.

Since some may suppose that government subsidies and aids were helpful in getting the railroads underway, and since a new era of subsidies portends, it will be well to begin the account with the building of the railroads and explore some of the varied effects of this before taking up regulation and control.

3 | Aiding the Railroads 1830-1871

THE BUILDING of the railroads in the United States was done almost entirely between 1830 and World War I. Such building as has been done since has consisted mostly of double-tracking, shortening routes, and building bridges. The first stage of railroading falls between the years 1830-1871, for in this period there was considerable governmental (Federal, state, and local) aid extended to get the building done. It did not entirely end in 1871; earlier grants were still available to some lines, but at that point governments turned their attention from aiding to regulating, restraining, and controlling the railroads. Animosity began to replace sympathy toward them. From the early 1830's into the 1850's most of the direct aid and efforts to facilitate their building came from state and local governments. After that, the Federal government became deeply involved in fostering railroad building. Since this early involvement had its effects and left a legacy, it will be well to examine into the whys, wheres, and consequences of it.

It is not apparent why governments became as involved as they did in early railroad building. The first decade or so of this activity coincided with the Age of Jackson. The main thrust of the Jacksonians was against special privileges to certain groups, against government aid for internal improvements, and in favor of leaving economic activities to the private initiative of the people. Jackson and most of his Democratic successors were concerned with disengaging government from the economy. One might suppose, then, that railroad builders would have been left to their own devices.

So they might have been if many of the Jacksonians had had their way. But the Jacksonian ascendancy was never so complete, nor were his Democratic followers so completely persuaded of the advantages of *laissez-faire*. In any case, theirs was a great wave going counter to the still deep-running tide of mercantilism. The Jacksonians (or Democrats) made up only one of the two major political parties of the time. The other party consisted of Whigs, and they were favorably disposed toward such mercantilistic carry-overs as government appropriations for internal improvements, the granting of monopolies, and such like.

States and local governments had long been accustomed to chartering roads, bridges, banks, and other types of semiprivate undertakings. Moreover, the early effort of the Jacksonians appears to have been aimed more at getting or keeping the Federal government out of such activities than changing state policies. The principle was by no means established that government should not intervene in economic activities. If there was a going principle, it was more nearly the one that government at some level should aid, at the least by granting a special charter and frequently by actually subsidizing, in developing transport.

Thoroughfares of Sorts

Early aid to the railroads becomes more readily understandable when they are considered as analogous to highways and waterways. Highways and waterways were usually thoroughfares, open to traffic of all comers, though tolls might sometimes be charged. Governments usually fostered thoroughfares in one way or another: sometimes building roads and canals, chartering them, granting them monopolies, and favoring them with the use of the power of eminent domain.

Railroad tracks were never thoroughfares to any extent; from first to last traffic on them was either monopolized or controlled by a single company. Yet they received many of the aids which thoroughfares received. Looking back on it, one may wonder why they were not treated as private undertakings, as factories were. The answer, in part, is that there was no tradition for roads to be treated in this way, and that railways were early conceived on an analogy with thoroughfares. They were something lying somewhere between a public thoroughfare and a private facility. Much mischief has followed from the ambiguity of this conception.

Of course, government aid to railroad building did not occur simply because of confusion about the nature of railroading. It may, indeed, have been the other way around: the nature of railroading may have been confused to facilitate government aid. At any rate, governments aided railroads because politicians perceived some advantage to be gained by such promotion. Sometimes that advantage was personal and direct, as when they received stock or other emoluments from promoters; at other times, it may have been indirect by way of facilities gained for some portion or all of their constituencies. Merchants, tradesmen, manufacturers, farmers, and what have you, wanted a railroad to and from their communities. The city fathers of one town wanted to gain for their locale a favorable position *vis à vis* their competitors elsewhere. Much of the history of railroads and government intervention can only be correctly construed in terms of commercial rivalries, competing locales, and the pulling and hauling between them for advantage. Those involved frequently turned to politicians to get them to use government to better their position. Since these contests are a major part of the context of the story from first to last, it will be useful to introduce them at this point.

Not all towns, nor all locales, nor every region, had the same interest in or pressing need for railroads. The political pressures were not equalized over the country. The topography varied; the population was unevenly distributed; and political advantage from promoting railroads was much greater in some areas than others. Government aid to railroads needs to be understood, then, within the historical and geographical background of these disparities.

A U.S. Common Market Tempts Government Aid

These United States became potentially a great common market with the ratification of the Constitution of 1787. States were generally forbidden to place obstacles in the way of commerce. This potential market had been extended far beyond the Appalachian Mountains by the Treaty of Paris of 1783, by the terms of which Britain recognized the Mississippi River as the western boundary of the United States. The bounds were extended all the way to the Rocky Mountains in 1803 by the Louisiana Purchase.

The key to the commercial opening up of this vast trans-Appalachian territory was transport. Who would receive the greatest benefit from such commerce as might develop would depend upon where the terminals of the trade routes were located. Thus it was that government aid for internal improvements, as road building and such like were then called, rather quickly became a major political issue. It was a heatedly debated national issue from the early years of the nineteenth century down to 1830, when Jackson virtually brought such Federal projects to a halt by his veto of the Maysville Road Bill.

Part of the impetus to finding ways to funnel the commerce from the American interior to the East Coast can be explained by the location of the bulk of the population and the character of the cities. According

The Bettmann Archive, Inc.

The first New York State railroad, the *Dewitt Clinton* of 1831, capable of the "frightful" speed of a mile in four minutes.

to calculations from the census of 1800, the population center of the United States was only a few miles south and west of Baltimore, Maryland. Most towns of any size were port towns, and, with the exception of New Orleans which was not then in the United States, these were all east of the mountains, on or near the Atlantic. The major port cities were Boston, Newport, New York City, Philadelphia, Baltimore, Norfolk, Wilmington, and Charleston.

To Save the Cities

The future growth and dominance of these cities was placed in jeopardy by the acquisition and opening up of the territory beyond the

Appalachian Mountains. Particularly was this true of the port cities from Baltimore northward. These had a narrow coastal hinterland to draw from within their own states or locales; the tidewater did not run far back, and mountains were relatively close to the sea. New York and Philadelphia were then the metropolitan centers, but anyone looking into the future would probably have predicted that they, along with other East Coast cities, would be dwarfed by cities in the Mississippi Valley which would send produce from that vast area to the rest of the world.

New York State, Pennsylvania, and Virginia had more pressing reasons than the other states to be concerned with the Appalachian barrier. Each of these states had considerable territory beyond the mountains within their boundaries. This situation was of greatest concern in New York and Pennsylvania. Most of New York lies west of the mountains, and Pennsylvania is cut in two by the Alleghenies. These states had internal political and economic reasons for trying to find commercial routes across the mountains in addition to the interests of the coastal cities. Both New York and Pennsylvania built thousands of miles of improved roads in the first three decades of the nineteenth century. Other areas induced the Federal government to undertake the construction of a national turnpike to connect the East with the Midwest.

All this flurry of building had little discernible effect on the flow of commerce. Many of the improved roads were commercial flops; it was still less expensive to float goods down the river from Pittsburgh to New Orleans than to haul them in wagons over the mountains. The steamboat opened up new possibilities for the use of the Ohio, Mississippi, and their river tributaries; by its use goods could not only be shipped downstream but upstream as well. The American cities of the future would probably be St. Louis and New Orleans, with lesser centers at such places as Pittsburgh, Cincinnati, and Memphis. A look at a topographical map of the United States should confirm that this was the most likely prospect.

If the traffic in goods had followed the course of the great interior rivers, if it had flowed from the Midwest into the Mid-South as it bade fair to do, the history of the United States would undoubtedly have been altered. If energy had been concentrated on making the rivers safer, if access to them had been opened up by roads, canals, and smaller streams, they might have served well for an extensive transport.

It may be too much of a speculation to think that such a linkage between North and South would have forestalled a civil war. Certainly, the peoples would have been bound closer together by this dependency. Of course, it did not work out that way.

The Canal Era

American ingenuity, eastern interests, the accident of state boundaries traversing the mountains, the concentration of population on the eastern side of the mountains with its determinative role in the use of political power, combined to produce a different result. The first major breakthrough in the effort to link the Midwest to the Northeast commercially was the Erie Canal. This canal was projected and built by the government of the state of New York to link Lake Erie to Albany by water. From Albany, traffic could readily flow down the Hudson to New York City. The building of the Erie was an amazing engineering feat in its day. It was completed during the 1820's, and became very quickly a commercial success. It is not too much to say that at the time New York City was saved as the leading port in the United States by the Erie Canal.

Not so, of course, the other port cities of the East; their prospects were dimmed by New York's triumph. So it was that the rush was on in other states to build canals, with similar triumphs envisioned. None of these undertakings was more ambitious than the one in Pennsylvania. It was to connect Pittsburgh with Philadelphia, providing a much shorter route than the one in New York to the Midwest. Unfortunately for Pennsylvanians, the topography between the two points was ill-suited to canal building. Undaunted by this, builders went ahead with the project. This is how they did it:

> From Philadelphia a railroad traversed the eighty-one miles to Columbia on the Susequehanna. From Columbia a canal ascended the Susquehanna and then traveled westward along the Juniata to Hollidaysburg, where the Allegheny ridge 2,291 feet high had to be surmounted. The device chosen was the Allegheny Portage Railroad, which mounted each side of the ridge with five inclined planes interspersed with level stretches. Stationary engines pulled the vehicles up the inclines; horses pulled them on the level tracks. In this fashion cars or cradles with canal boats were raised from the Juniata and finally let

> down on the other side into the Conemaugh at Johnstown, whence a canal continued along the routes of various rivers to Pittsburgh.[1]

Even after such an effort, it was not attended with much success in attaining its object. Most of the Midwestern traffic still went by way of the Erie. There was much more canal building, however. A Chesapeake and Ohio canal was projected to link Virginia and Maryland with the Ohio River, but it was never completed. Several Midwestern states sunk large amounts of funds into canal building in the 1830's and 1840's. Indeed, some of them extended their credit so far that when the depression came they forfeited payment or went bankrupt. These failures considerably dampened the enthusiasm in some states for government ventures in subsidizing transportation facilities, and proponents of *laissez-faire* were strengthened.

The Urge to Subsidize

But if there was ever a notion that dies hard (that is, does not die), it is the notion that government should subsidize or otherwise sponsor some industry or undertaking. It dies hard because there are those ready to hand to benefit personally from such aid and who will use their ingenuity to bring forward reasons that will convince the public of some general benefit forthcoming. So it was, at least, with transportation.

The era of canal building was not over before the era of railroad building began in earnest. Nor can it be said that overmuch had been learned from the debacles in canal building following upon government involvement. For cities on the East Coast, the railroad offered the possibility of competing with New York City in tapping the Midwest. The railroad might do for Philadelphia and Pennsylvania what their canal had not. Thus it was that during "the period 1840 to 1853, the city and county governments in Pennsylvania contributed about $14 million to railways. Philadelphia alone incurred a debt of over $8 million, about $20 per person, for railways. In 1852, $6,750,000 of the Pennsylvania Railroad's total capitalization of $9,876,000 had been contributed by local governments."[2]

---

[1] Edward C. Kirkland, *A History of American Life* (New York: Appleton-Century-Crofts, 1951, 3rd ed.), p. 236.

[2] Gilbert C. Fite and Jim E. Reese, *An Economic History of the United States* (Boston: Houghton Mifflin, 1965, 2nd ed.), p. 199.

Governments in other states engaged in some of the same kind of activity. The "merchants of Baltimore had conceived the . . . ambitious enterprise of a railroad across the Allegheny Mountains to the Ohio River. Private subscriptions to its shares having proved inadequate to its financial requirements, resort was had to the city of Baltimore and to the state of Maryland, whose credit therefor was utilized to the extent of $5,000,000."[3] Even New York State inhabitants were soon worried by the railroad, for that mode of transport soon demonstrated its general superiority over canals and inland waterways (not by cheaper rates but because of schedule predictability and year round use). "By 1840, the state of New York had granted its credit in aid of railroad companies to the amount of nearly $4,000,000, and eventually the aid of this character from the state and from counties and municipalities reached the sum of $40,000,000."[4]

Some of the early eastern lines were actually state projects. "In Pennsylvania two of the earliest lines in the state, the Portage Railroad and the Philadelphia and Columbia, were constructed with state money, as was the strategically located Western and Atlantic in Georgia."[5] More common, however, was financial assistance from states or municipalities to otherwise private building. One historian sums up government aid in the East in this way: "The Western Railroad in Massachusetts, the Erie in New York, the Baltimore & Ohio in Maryland, and most of the railroads in Virginia were among the rail recipients of state assistance."[6]

Several Midwestern states also assisted railroad building extensively. Ohio adopted a law which committed the state to furnish one-third of the capital for any railroad company. "In 1837, the state of Illinois appropriated over $10,000,000 to public improvements; a debt of $34.10 for each person in the state. . . . In 1838, the state made an additional appropriation of $9,000,000. . . . Missouri spent over $30,000,000 with only $6,000,000 of assets to show for it; Michigan incurred an immense liability without adequate security. . . ."[7]

States aided railroads in other ways than by subsidies and loans. As

---

[3] Henry S. Haines, *Problems in Railway Regulation* (New York: Macmillan, 1911), p. 178.

[4] *Ibid.,* p. 181.

[5] Stover, *op. cit.,* p. 30.

[6] *Ibid.,* p. 31.

[7] Haines, *op. cit.,* pp. 181-82.

a general rule, railroads were, at the least, chartered by states. Sometimes these charters included monopoly privileges. In some instances, exemptions from state taxes would be granted, and they were usually given privileges in the use of eminent domain for the acquiring of land. It is safe to say that virtually all the railroad trackage laid in the country was laid in consequence of some special privilege not granted to all enterprises.

States Rush in Where Individuals Fear to Tread

At the same time, it needs to be emphasized that there were great differences in the character and extent of this aid. Much, probably most, extended only to chartering and allowing the railroads to acquire land by eminent domain. Of the rest, there were some loans, land grants, and monetary grants—each of these quite different in character. As to financing, this judgment is undoubtedly correct: "Most of the money for the early railroads came from private investors."[8]

Even so, such government aid left some unpleasant consequences in its wake. Government aid was extended on the grounds that private investors would not put up sufficient money for building the roads at the time. The meaning of this is that men who have money to invest do not judge such building to have the best prospect for returns, that money can be better used elsewhere. Though private investors may be wrong, they are the experts in the field. Governments are betting against the field when they put up money. Even if government ventures are superficially successful on occasion, the success is frequently marred by unwanted consequences.

In any case, the state aid to railroads proved to be the wrong way to get them built. One historian sums up the results to the midpoint of the nineteenth century: "The experience of . . . states with government-sponsored internal improvements—the Erie being the sole exception—had ended disastrously."[9] Another writer notes that "there was a good deal of fraud and corruption in connection with state aid to railroads, and in later years a number of states repudiated some of their obligations made in connection with railroad construction. Because of the corrup-

---

[8] Stover, *op. cit.,* p. 31.

[9] Robert S. Hunt, *Law and Locomotives* (Madison: State Historical Society of Wisconsin, 1958), p. 38.

tion involved and because of the heavy tax burden the people were asked to bear to meet the states' promises, it later became common for state constitutions to prohibit the investment of state money in any private enterprise."[10]

It often turned out that what was not a good investment for private investors was not a good one for governments. But that is not the whole story. Government investment made such railroad building politically determined rather than economic, turned over the funds to the cleverest lobbyists on occasion rather than to those likely to provide sound management, led to building at times and to places that would not then be justified, and sometimes saddled these premature undertakings with large debts. By reserving the right to regulate in charters, and by giving aid, states set the stage for intervention and made the status of the railroads before the law ambiguous.

Federal Entry in 1850's

The debacle wrought by state intervention did not long deter the Federal government from entering the field. The Federal government began the move toward subsidizing in the 1850's, and then with Southern representatives out of the Congress during the Civil War plunged headlong into sponsoring railroad building. Though some land grants were made in some of the states of the Midwest and South, the most extensive Federal aid was given to the transcontinental routes. Hence, attention can most profitably be focused on them.

The background to the transcontinentals is this: The United States acquired California from Mexico in 1848. A couple of years before, title to the vast Oregon country had been made certain by treaty with Britain. Almost immediately proposals began to be made in Congress for the building of a railroad to the Pacific. There were two main reasons for the matter to come before the national government. A transcontinental railroad would have to go through territory not then organized into states, territory over which the United States government had sole authority. Secondly, it was a project of such dimensions that there was little hope that the states standing to benefit directly from it would undertake its construction. The location of the route for such a road was a political

---

[10] Russell E. Westmeyer, *Economics of Transportation* (Englewood Cliffs: Prentice-Hall, 1952), pp. 47-48.

issue for most of the 1850's. The pressure for a southern route led to the Gadsden Purchase in 1853, and that for a Midwestern one led to the Kansas-Nebraska Act of 1854. Even so, no project was actually authorized until the war was well under way.

With the South out of the Union, Congress authorized a transcontinental railroad that would have its eastern terminus in the Midwest. Two companies were to build railroads—the Union Pacific and the Central Pacific. To facilitate such building, the government granted lands, made some loans, and enabled them to borrow money with government backing. Subsequently, lands were granted and aid given for the building of other transcontinentals, the most extensive for the Northern Pacific Railroad.

Clarifying Some Facts

It is important, again, that the extent and character of this aid be made clear. Historians, and others, have frequently exaggerated the extent and implied that the railroads got great benefits at the expense of the rest of the country. It is much to the point that the lands granted were worth little to nothing on the market at the time they were granted. The railroads built through them greatly augmented their value. The lands were parceled out so that the company got one section and the government kept one in alternating parcels. Thus, the benefits from the appreciation of land values due to the railroads were apportioned between the roads and the government. In the case of loans, they were largely repaid in one way or another over the years (with interest). Nor were the Federal land grants extended to most railroads. "Such grants were made in aid of a total of 18,738 miles of railroad line—less than 8 per cent of the total mileage of railroads built in the United States."[11]

Even so, it does not follow that such aid as was given was prudent, and it is certain that there were ramifying consequences which few would have willed. The biggest scandal that occurred involved the building of the Union Pacific Railroad; the events surrounding this will give an indication of some of these consequences.

The Union Pacific was assigned the task of building the road from the Midwest westward to junction with the line being built eastward by the

[11] Robert S. Henry, "The Railroad Land Grant Legend in American History Texts," *Issues in American Economic History*, Gerald D. Nash, ed. (Boston: D. C. Heath, 1964), p. 324.

Central Pacific. To facilitate this building, the Federal government granted lands, authorized the use of timber and fill dirt from the public domain, and provided loans by way of government bonds. Initially, these loans were to be secured by a first mortgage against the railroad, but they were later reduced to second mortgage status. Congress required that at least minimal investments be made from private funds before the undertaking should get under way.

Crédit Mobilier

One might suppose that with all this aid, private financiers would have adjudged the Union Pacific to be a good investment. They did not. The government bonds could only be disposed of at a considerable discount. One of the men involved testified that there were "very few capitalists who had faith enough in the successful prosecution of the undertaking to feel it was safe to invest a dollar in the bonds, or even to take the notes of the company, with bonds as collateral, at 60 cents on the dollar without a large commission." Moreover, as a recent study points out, "the market situation of the Union Pacific's stock was even weaker than that of the bonds. John Duff asserted that Union Pacific stock could not be sold 'except to people who would take a risk as they would at a faro-bank.' "[12] True, much of this testimony was self-interested, but other indications are that the future earnings of the Union Pacific were not then viewed as such that heavy investment was warranted.

Even the directors of the company plowed most of their investment into a construction company—Crédit Mobilier—rather than the Union Pacific. They clearly judged that if there was profit to be made, it was from construction rather than from operating the railroad.

An exposé of Crédit Mobilier began in 1872 with the publication of damaging letters in the New York *Sun,* and the matter was brought to national attention by a congressional investigation. There were two facets to this scandal. The one that probably made the biggest impact at the time was that several members of Congress had bought stock in the construction company at par value. The stock turned out to be worth much more. It was charged that the stock had been sold to them at this price in order to influence votes. The other was that the well-situated

[12] Robert W. Fogel, *The Union Pacific Railroad* (Baltimore: The Johns Hopkins Press, 1960), p. 76.

directors of the Union Pacific had made an inordinate profit from construction, leaving the parent company in bad financial condition. It is the burden of a recent study to show that the profits were not exorbitant in view of the risks.[13] More importantly, this study indicates that even if the construction company had charged much less for construction, the Union Pacific would still have been too deeply in debt to make a go of it. The discounting of stocks and bonds made the enterprise too costly in the first place. Secondly, "it was the unbearable weight of its obligations to the government that finally forced the road into receivership in 1893."[14]

A Trail of Disaster

Premature railroad building induced by government grants left a trail of disaster in its wake. The ramifying consequences are too extensive to be gone into in detail here. They can only be partially suggested. Government aid fostered a boom in railroad building that extended beyond those railroads receiving it. There was overbuilding in some areas; many roads were left in shaky financial conditions; there were bankruptcies. Hapless settlers were lured by government and railroads to buy farms in the semi-arid West; many would return eastward after years of failure. Unscrupulous financiers moved into railroading, sometimes made their quick profits, then left the railroads in disarray. Boom towns founded on some illusive prospect of wealth or future greatness were hurriedly built, only to be deserted when the bubble burst. Nor should it be forgotten that the wholesale slaying of the buffalo and the destructive Indian wars of the 1870's were offshoots of the railroad boom, along with the influx of homesteaders that disrupted ranching. There is every reason to believe that America would have had such a railroad system as was needed and could have been afforded without the government aid and without the manifold infelicities that accompanied premature building.

Indeed, most of the railroad track in the country was laid after governments had withdrawn all but minimal aid in nearly all cases. In 1870, there were only 52,000 miles of track; by 1910, it exceeded 200,000 miles. The Federal government did not make new land grants after 1871, though some of those already granted continued to be appropriated. In

---

[13] See *ibid.,* passim.

[14] *Ibid.,* p. 88.

the 1880's some of the lands conditionally granted began to be reclaimed by the government.

The railroads generally survived the effects of government aid for premature building. Builders continued to build; systems were knit together; many private entrepreneurs learned to operate them so as to provide profit for investors and benefits to consumers. Service was greatly improved in the latter part of the nineteenth century and rates were brought down. Goods from the far corners of the United States flowed into cities and American ports and thence all over the world.

Governments began to change their policies, too, though it was hardly for the better. They were barely done with fostering premature building with its unwanted consequences when they turned to harassment. Indeed, there had been some harassment by local governments from the beginning, but the pace quickened in the 1870's, and it was only another decade before the Federal government would turn its restrictive power on the railroads. It is time now to explore this about-face.

4 | The Thrust to Regulation

THE COURTSHIP of the railroads by government ended rather abruptly in the 1870's. Not only were the governmental favors reduced or shut off but governments began to turn their energies to regulating, controlling, restricting, and containing the railroads. True, there had been some opposition to railroads from the beginning which resulted in some restrictive legislation: there were early fears that the human body could not withstand such tremendous speeds as 15 to 20 miles per hour; farmers' fields were sometimes ignited by sparks from train engines; cattle owners resented the threat the moving steam engine posed to their herds; and some people resented the trains running on Sunday. Some states passed fencing laws, and some communities would not allow trains to pass through on the Sabbath.

But, in the main, the people of the United States wanted railroads, and their governments responded by offering various aids and inducements to railroad building, as has been shown. The policies began a major shift in the 1870's, and they were probably accelerated by the Crédit Mobilier exposures. Communities still wanted railroad service, but they turned from inducement to compulsion to get it. In the course of time, railroads became, in the eyes of some, Public Enemy Number One.

What brought on this about-face? Did railroad rates skyrocket once the public's dependence on this mode of transportation was established? Was service refused to some and reduced to others? Did the railroads cease improving their equipment once they were built? Did the railroads fail to expand markets, to bring goods at competitive prices from distant points, or provide a world market for American farm produce?

In general, each of these questions must be answered in the negative. A survey of the situation in the latter part of the nineteenth century—the period when the clamor for government intervention was mounting but before such control had been generally instituted—provides impressive evidence of the benefits of the railroads to the American public. Despite the great handicaps under which many of the railroads had been or were being built and operated—such handicaps as heavy indebtedness, haphazard construction fostered by fickle legislation, overbuilding promoted by political expedience, the invitation that government aid and the possibilities of suborning legislatures offered to sharp operators, the technological difficulties of a new means of transportation, the immensity of America and the unfriendliness of much of its terrain and weather—almost all indications are that the railroads were doing a good job.

Energetic entrepreneurs put together great railroad systems out of the hodgepodge of short lines that had been built, linking great cities and providing far-flung services for the hinterlands. So it was with such systems as the Pennsylvania, New York Central, Southern, Chicago, Burlington, and Quincy, Atchison, Topeka, and Santa Fe. James J. Hill wrought the Great Northern with private funds and succeeded in competition with the heavily subsidized Northern Pacific.

Railroad equipment was improved as new technology became available, and service was usually bettered by these improvements. Steel rails replaced wood and iron; flanges were placed on wheels rather than on the rails; passenger coaches with aisles down the middle became standard; sleeping cars were introduced and steadily improved; air brakes and signaling devices added greatly to the safety of the railroads. Interchange arrangements were frequently worked out with other shippers, though initially railroads were sometimes chary of cooperating with one another. The railroads were the instigators of a standard time within time zones for the whole United States, a system that was much later prescribed by the Federal government. That privately-owned railroads were generally improving the quality and extent of their service should be beyond doubt.

Rail Rates Were Declining

As far as rail rates were concerned, they usually declined from the 1870's to the early twentieth century. Only in three years—1878, 1880, and 1883—was there a counter movement in freight rates. In 1868, the average railway revenue per ton mile was over 1.9 cents; by 1900, this had been reduced to only a little more than .7 cents.[1] Of the benefits of the railroad to wheat farmers in opening up markets to them, one book has this information: "Mr. Edward Atkinson has estimated at 66 cents the saving effected from 1873 to 1887 in the cost of growing a bushel of wheat in the United States, carrying it 1,200 to 1,500 miles by rail, and by lake and rail, to the Atlantic seaboard and thence by vessel to Liverpool. Not less than 50 per cent of that saving Mr. Atkinson attributed to the reduction made in the charge for carrying the wheat to the Atlantic, 25 per cent to the reduction in the charges for ocean transportation, and only 10 per cent to the reduction brought about in the cost of planting and harvesting."[2] Andrew Carnegie was, in part, remarking the marvelous impact of the railroad, when he said: "To make a ton of steel one and a half tons of iron stone has to be mined, transported by rail a hundred miles to the lakes, carried by boat hundreds of miles, transferred to cars, transported by rail one hundred and fifty miles to Pittsburgh. . . . How then could steel be manufactured and sold without loss at three pounds for two cents? This, I confess, seemed to me incredible . . . but it was so."[3]

Of course, the greatest benefits from rail service went to consumers, both domestic and foreign—that is, to virtually everyone. Americans quickly became accustomed to having on the shelves of their stores products from all over America and from much of the rest of the world. They not only could have them with great predictability, but they could also have them much cheaper than ever before in the latter part of the nineteenth century. The decline in rail rates was measured by the consumer in the general decline of prices, a decline that was sometimes absolute and at others relative to wages.

Why, then, was the political power of the state and Federal governments turned against the railroads? That power is traced from and responsible to the American people. And, the American people were surely the beneficiaries of the railroads. The explanation is that some portion of the American people did not see it or understand it this way, that they

---

[1] Fite and Reese, *op. cit.*, p. 334.

[2] Hugo R. Meyer, *Government Regulation of Railway Rates* (New York: Macmillan, 1906), pp. 212-13.

[3] Fite and Reese, *op. cit.*, p. 294.

had come to view the matter from other angles than their common interest as consumers. Much underlay the thrust to regulation, but what was involved can be reduced to and treated under five headings.

1. *Opposition to Big Business*

The railroads were among the first large corporations in the United States. In the 1870's several had or were to become giants, doing business across the lines of several states or territories and extending their tracks over whole regions. These great corporations owned thousands (or even millions) of acres of land, numerous freight and passenger stations, thousands of miles of track, and thousands of pieces of rolling stock. They frequently bought out smaller railroads and extended their facilities into new areas or covered more fully the old. By cooperation with one another the railroads were providing nationwide transportation facilities, and in their wake other businesses became nationwide, spearheaded by Standard Oil.

Americans have long been ambiguous in their attitudes toward and treatment of big businesses. They have patronized them, else they would not have become big businesses. Those who live in towns or cities where corporations are headquartered take pride in their edifices and the number employed is often a local boast. Men seek employment with large corporations, for they observe that pay is better and jobs more secure. Yet, Americans often bestow their vote on those who claim that they will bring the corporations to heel, who describe them as irresponsible leviathans which must be regulated and controlled, who engage in antibusiness demagoguery. A double standard of behavior when applied to economic and political realms appears to be involved.

A part of this animosity toward big business can most likely be ascribed to just plain human cussedness. People quite often like to think of the mighty being brought low, are jealous of the successful, and behave inconsistently and irresponsibly at the ballot box. (Where is there a greater lure to irresponsible behavior than in voting? Men may vote for the demagogue who appeals most breathlessly to their prejudices and then denounce politicians for their inconstancy and venality.) Moreover, people are apt to be suspicious of anything large, removed from their direct surveillance, and whose workings they do not understand. Thus, they are ready enough, in the main, to believe the worst of large businesses.

The opposition to and fear of the railroads did, however, have a particular historical setting. The growth of large railroad corporations was paralleled by the growth of other large businesses. In the last two decades or so of the nineteenth century, it appeared, or could be made to appear, that consolidation was leading toward the domination of whole industries by single companies. While this did not immediately portend for the railways, a similar result might be achieved by pooling, or so it was feared. Nationwide industries were something which Americans had not yet much experienced. Would energetic companies squeeze out all competitors and be in position to practice extortion on the American people? That such a view did not take into account the exigencies of business, the potential role of competitors in the free market, or what it would be most profitable for a business to do, does not mean that it could not be believed. What would happen in most industries would be that once one company had shown how to provide goods or services on a nationwide scale, others soundly financed and well managed would follow in their path. So it happened in the oil industry, and many another.

Meanwhile, critics turned the searchlight on the railway industry and found in their practices—whether innocent or not so innocent but, whichever, determinedly misunderstood—dangers to the republic and potentialities for spreading evil. Traffic associations and pools would permit the railroads to act monopolistically. Rate differentials between large and small shippers were prejudicial to the "little man." The railroads issued many free passes, and these were described as efforts to suborn public leaders and officials. Railroads sometimes "discriminated" by charging more for a short haul than for a long haul. Even competition, when it resulted in lowering of rates, was frequently described as ruinous and dangerous. Examination into the basis of railway practices will be taken up later, but the point here is that they were described in such a way that some came to think of the railroads as a menace to be contained.

2. *The Ambiguous Legal Status*

The railroads have paid, and continue to pay, an excessively extortionate price for the early favors received from governments and, what is more to the point, so have and do the shipping and traveling and consuming public. This latter point needs to be kept ever in mind. Governmental agents can conceive of all sorts of devices by which to penalize and constrain railroads, but they have hit upon none, to my knowledge, which have not been passed on in one way or another to the public. Even so, governments have beset the railroads with all sort of taxes, regulations, restrictions, and controls. The bases for part of these were the favors granted and for much of the rest the ambiguous status that these confirmed.

The railroads were bred in legal ambiguity, developed in limbo, and have languished in a maze of regulation and restriction which was issued on the basis of this dubious status. Law in the United States, with the exception of Louisiana, is a combination of the common law—that is, English practice, immemorial custom, precedents set by judicial decision—and legislative enactments. In the absence of specific constitutional provision and subsequent legislative enactment, the common law generally prevails. The common law is itself a wondrous maze of judicial decisions reaching back to the dim English past and threading through the centuries in any particular matter amidst changing cultural patterns. It embraces both relics of feudal serfdom and modern contractual relations of free men.

Railroads were chartered as corporations. The corporation arose as a medieval device by which various groups were authorized and granted privileges and immunities. Its most obvious use was the chartering of towns and communities as political units, a practice continued by the states in America. Corporations were, then, governmental or semigovernmental in character. Railroad corporations had some of the residues of this governmental character, since they could, under court supervision, exercise the power of eminent domain. The getting of a charter involved the tacit or explicit acknowledgment of the authority of the sovereign—in this case, the state—to lay down rules for the operation of the corporation. The charters of railroads usually either spelled out such rules or reserved the privilege to regulate rates, and so forth. Historically, charters had frequently been given for such undertakings as bridges and roads. The public was said to have a special interest in these; they often had monopolies; and their fees were subject to supervision.

The public or private status of the railroads was further confused by aids granted for their building. That railroads should receive land grants, use the credit of government, or be subsidized certainly implied that they had a different public character from that of, say, farms.

The railroads, it turned out, were not thoroughfares, not necessarily nor particularly monoplies, nor once they were finished with the power of eminent domain were they governmental. A doctrine was exhumed from the past to define their legal status. It is the doctrine, as we know it, that they are common carriers. This doctrine has its roots in the Middle Ages in the notion that certain sorts of undertakings are common callings. As one writer describes the matter, "For some reason that is not entirely clear certain of these common callings, including the services of innkeepers, wharfingers, ferrymen, and carriers were singled out for special consideration by the courts, and a body of court decisions grew up limiting the freedom of action of individuals engaged in these businesses."[4] The common carrier doctrine as it took shape required those who undertook to serve in this capacity to serve all comers on equal terms and at reasonable rates, among other things. (There were, of course, protective limits to the service that had to be provided.) The implicit serfdom here is appropriate to the time of its origins and helps to account for some of the resentment customers of the railroads encounter from personnel. Americans, at least, do not like to be made to serve, but welcome the opportunity when they are free to do so or not.

The stage was set for bringing these medieval relics into play by the acts of incorporation and aids granted to the railroads. Even so, they might have been permitted to continue to atrophy, as they were for a time. From the early years of railroad building into the 1870's the tendency in the United States was away from medieval and mercantilistic practices toward full-fledged private property in provision of goods and services, toward competition and away from chartered monopolies, toward allowing prices to be set in the free market, toward making the privileges of incorporation available to all by general acts of legislatures. Railroad historians generally agree that states did not much exercise their powers of regulation and that when they early attempted to do so they either abandoned the attempts or did not pursue them vigorously. With the abandonment of extensive aid in the 1870's, the railroads might have become fully the private property of their owners to use as they saw fit, subject only to general laws and such specific ones as might be necessary for public safety. In the 1880's the Supreme Court confirmed this direc-

---

[4] Westmeyer, *op. cit.,* p. 94.

tion by declaring that corporate property was property in the meaning of the Fourteenth Amendment and protected by it.

Once the hue and cry was raised against the railroads, the relics in the common law served as a basis for regulation. The charges against the

Union Pacific Railroad Museum Collection

The *General Sherman,* a woodburner, was built in 1864-65 in Paterson, N.J. It was brought by steamboat to Omaha in June, 1965.

railroads acquired much of their force from the supposed public character of the roads. What the railroads charged and the service they provided would be only the affair of contracting parties if they were fully private; if they were semipublic (or however it should be described), their charges would be of public interest and might be publicly determined. When the Supreme Court decided in the 1880's that the so-called Granger laws regulating railroads were invalid for interstate shipments, an additional basis for regulation was supplied by the commerce clause of the United States Constitution. None of these laws or precedents or constitutional provisions caused the regulation of the railroads; instead, they served as a legal basis for the action and added impetus to the thrust to regulation by supporting the notion that railroad practices were of public concern.

3. *Political Face-Saving*

It became politically advantageous to be against the railroads in the latter part of the nineteenth century. This did not come about so much at first because of public opposition to the railroads as because of public distrust of politicians. For several decades scandal after scandal occurred as a result of government grants to railroads. The culmination came nationally with the Crédit Mobilier revelations, which were associated with other scandals of the Grant Administration as well as those of Reconstruction state and local governments. Politics and politicians were very nearly discredited for many Americans. How deeply politicians became mired in scandal is illustrated by this example from Wisconsin in the 1850's involving a projected railroad:

> With eight exceptions—those who were to benefit in other ways—each legislator who voted for the bill received a package containing the promised amount of La Crosse and Milwaukee securities. A few who had rendered special services, such as Senator Hadley and Assemblyman Falvey, received more than their colleagues. In addition, the comptroller, the lieutenant-governor, the chief and assistant clerks of the Assembly, and the governor's private secretary also received five or ten thousand dollars in securities. Kilbourn had a package of ten thousand dollars worth of bonds prepared for Judge Abram D. Smith of the Supreme Court, and Governor Bashford got fifty thousand dollars worth. The two senators and twelve assemblymen who did not vote received no package. Six senators and seven assemblymen refused the bonds and voted against the bill.[5]

Such scandals not only reflected on the individuals involved but upon the profession of politician itself.

Much of the public ire was turned on the politicians initially, though of course the bribers were guilty along with the bribed. The "scoundrels" were sometimes turned out of office wholesale in states. Constitutions were adopted which greatly restricted state grants and aids to businesses. Legislative acts sometimes doubled the penalties for bribery when committed by public officials.

But there was another route politicians could take to save face and

---

[5] Hunt, *op. cit.,* p. 14.

reclaim some public respect. It was to shift the onus from politics to business, to expose businessmen as malefactors and reveal politicians as guardian angels. Possibly, no one thought it out in such all encompassing fashion. In fact, however, such a shift did occur. What an individual politician could do would be to vote against the railroads and establish his innocence of bribery. A vote to contain, obstruct, and restrict big business could be worn as a badge of innocence.

4. *Interest Group Support*

The thrust to regulation gained ground by focusing attention on the impact of the railroads on particular groups, locales, and regions rather than upon the general interest—i.e., that of consumers. Group was ranged against group, interest against interest, community against community, and region against region. Historians have often written as if the situation were one in the latter part of the nineteenth century in which the railroads were pitted against the general welfare of the United States. This is nonsense; the already indicated benefits to consumers proves the contrary. Nor were big businesses pitted in class array against the general welfare. They were much more apt to be pitted against one another in ways beneficial to the rest of the country; anyone who will take off the Marxian blinders can ascertain this for himself.

But to say that railroads benefited everyone as consumers is not to say that all were benefited equally, and they certainly did not benefit all producers and distributors and communities equally. There was the rub! When the railroads were being built, the merchants, manufacturers, farmers, and the people of an area in general had great hopes for what the railroad would do for them. Those in small communities had visions that their villages would become trading centers, manufacturing and mining centers, centers of art and culture, and even great cities. One railroad historian describes the spread of such notions this way:

> The inception and progress of the [railroad] fever came in time to have a pattern. First, some up-and-coming individual, or simply a fanatical dreamer, said forcibly that what his home town of Brownsville needed, if it were to share in America's great destiny, was a steam railroad. He talked the idea to anyone in Brownsville who would listen or could not get away, and the more he talked . . . , the better the idea seemed to him. It grew and blossomed and burgeoned and even soared. . . .

> It also dripped with gold, gold for all of Brownsville, soon to be a mighty metropolis, teeming with commerce, with industry, with the stir and bustle of countless travelers.[6]

Such dreams did sometimes become realities. Some villages did become metropolises, aided by the railroad. One could name, off hand, Chicago, Denver, St. Paul, Atlanta, Kansas City, and Fort Worth. But for most of them it was an impossible dream. The railroad was built through the town, but it remained what it was before—a small town. The fault, it was alleged, lay with railroad practices, particularly the differential in rates to localities. If Social Circle, Georgia, could have the same rate from New York as Atlanta (such a case was once heard), it, too, might become a great trading center.

Small towns were not the only ones in which there was interest in manipulating rates to local advantage. New York City exporters wanted to maintain their favorable position in relation to other eastern ports. Eastern ports wanted as good or better rates from the railroads for midwestern produce as Gulf ports. An early study of the cases brought before the Interstate Commerce Commission indicates that in case after case it was business interests within communities ranged against the railroads. The author concluded that "in most of the cases brought before the Commission the conflict has not been between the railways and the people, but between one section of the public and another section of the public, each such section being served by its particular railway or railways."[7] The railroads were, of course, caught in the middle. Generations of historians have taught that it was railroad discrimination against poor western farmers that produced the Granger laws. Recently, a historian has rediscovered the fact that proposals for rate-law reforms, "sponsored for the most part by merchants and businessmen, can scarcely be interpreted as agrarian attacks upon the business community. On the contrary, they were designed to protect vested commercial interests. . . ."[8] Or, I might add, to promote certain commercial interests.

A new order of political priorities existed, then, once the railroads were largely built. When railroads were being projected, the politician's

---

[6] Stewart H. Holbrook, *The Story of American Railroads* (New York: Crown, 1947), p. 40.

[7] Meyer, *op. cit.*, p. 337.

[8] George H. Miller, "Origins of the Iowa Granger Law," in Harry N. Scheiber, ed., *United States Economic History* (New York: Alfred A. Knopf, 1964), p. 311.

advantage lay with getting railroads built into the area where his constituents lived. Once the railroads were built, the pressure was on the politician to use political power to secure an advantage for his constituents from the railroads. If only one reason could be given for the thrust to regulation, this would be it.

5. *Socialist Ideas*

However, it is doubtful that local chambers of commerce, special interests of local producers and distributors, or communities ranged against one another could have brought off and maintained the sustained political assault on the railroads. They would need allies, and they got them. After all, the quest of businessmen for special advantage is easily unmasked as vulgar self-interest. Any political cause that is advanced for a considerable period of time requires a rhetoric which will give it the ring of nobility. The rhetoric for this cause was provided by socialism.

Socialists could, and did, link together the various thrusts and provide ideological foundations for them. Socialists were at the forefront of those denouncing big business. Marx, and others, had proclaimed that businesses would grow bigger and bigger until all competition had been extinguished. Despite the brave progressive talk, socialism contains a large measure of nostalgia for medieval practices in which property was not quite private; hence, it could and did subsume such doctrines as that of a common calling. Socialists read the whole conflict in terms of class conflict, gave politicians a rhetoric, and allowed them to appear noble when they advanced the special interests of their constituents, or tried to do so. Above all, socialism provided the egalitarian emphasis in terms of which railroad practices appeared to be unfair.

How socialism entered the stream of American politics is too complicated and abstruse to be told in detail here. Tiny socialist groups were being organized by the 1870's. Socialist ideas informed such labor organizations as the Knights of Labor. The Grange and the Farmer's Alliance at least provided organizations within which the ideas could be spread. Third parties, such as the Greenbackers and the Populists, were definitely under the influence of socialist ideas. Various intellectuals, utopians, and reformers helped to give voice to ideas drawn from socialism. From these varied sources they came to influence American political action.

The railroads were the leading villain of radicals in the latter part of the nineteenth century. The following is an indictment of them by a man who frequently lectured for the National Farmer's Alliance. He said that "the railroads are now menacing the peace and prosperity of the country in a far more grave and dangerous manner than was thought of by the people a half-century ago. Their power to centralize population, to control the commerce of the country, to build up a city or tear it down, to prosper one businessman and ruin another, to control legislatures and Congress, to pack courts, is what the people have come to fear."[9]

Senator William Peffer described the situation of the farmer in this way in 1891:

> . . . The railroad builder took the initiative. Close by his side was the money changer. The first took possession of the land, the other took possession of the farmer. One compelled the settler to pay the price fixed upon the railroad lands by the railroad; the other compelled the settler on the public lands within the grant to pay the increased price, and to borrow money through him to make the payments on both. This system continued until the farmer, accommodating himself to prevailing conditions, was in the hands of his destroyers.[10]

General James B. Weaver, Populist candidate for President in 1892, belabored the railroads in this fashion:

> In their delirium of greed the managers of our transportation systems disregard both private right and public welfare. Today they will combine and bankrupt their weak rivals, and by the expenditure of a trifling sum possess themselves of properties which cost the outlay of millions. Tomorrow they will capitalize their booty for five times the cost, issue their bonds, and proceed to levy tariffs upon the people to pay dividends upon the fraud.[11]

The doings of certain railroad financiers have long been the stock-in-trade stories of reformers. Here is Thomas E. Watson, another Populist, declaiming against Collis P. Huntington and Leland Stanford for allegedly taking funds from their company for nefarious ends:

---

[9] N. B. Ashby, "Transportation," in Irwin Unger, ed., *Populism: Nostalgic or Progressive* (The Berkeley Series, 1964), p. 27.

[10] Quoted in Vincent P. De Santis, *et al.*, *American Past and Present* (Boston: Allyn and Bacon, 1968), II, 185.

[11] Thomas A. Bailey, ed., *The American Spirit* (Boston: D. C. Heath, 1963), II, 520.

> It's not all they took, by a jug full.
>
> At this good hour Huntington, instead of being behind the bars as a convicted thief, is one of the Grandees of Plutocracy, and Stanford, instead of being in jail, is in the United States Senate!
>
> Of course, had these men stolen a bunch of cattle, they would have been shot down without ceremony. . . .
>
> But they showed better judgment.
>
> They stole enough to buy Judges, corrupt Legislators, and muzzle the Press.[12]

Those who would use governmental power to control the railroads, then, took the attention away from the benefits of the railroads to focus upon railroad practices. In order to evaluate their charges and the potentialities for harm in the fears they raised, it will be helpful to examine into the economics of railroading. This will provide a basis, also, from which to explore the impact of intervention.

---

[12] Paul Glad, ed., *The Process of American History* (Englewood Cliffs: Prentice-Hall, 1969), p. 144.

5 The Nature of Railroading

THERE WERE TWO basic charges against the railroads which promoted the increasing government regulation and control over the years. One was that they *discriminated* among their customers, particularly among shippers, and that this discrimination resulted in unjust rates. Specifically, critics claimed that the railroads favored those making large shipments over those making small ones, that they charged more for some short hauls than they did for long ones, that they gave preferential rates to some cities and denied them to others, that they gave rebates to strategically situated shippers, and that they gave free passes to influential persons to ride passenger trains. These practices were said to be unjust because they meant that small shippers, those living in cities or towns without preferential rates, farmers, and people without influence were not only paying their own way but were also subsidizing favored customers.

The second charge against the railroads was that *competition* among them was *imperfect*. Some locations were served by several railroads and might have, in addition, water transport available, while others would be served by only one railroad. Those who were served by competing lines benefited from lower rates, while those with only one line between points were charged what the traffic would bear. Of course, this was only the simplest level of the charge about competition. Reformers have actually been quite ambivalent toward it; if it does not exist, they picture the customer at the mercy of a single company; if it does exist, they are apt to describe with horror the competitive practices. The legislation fostered over the years reflects the ambivalence of the reformers toward competition. At any rate, they charged that competing railroads formed pools to divide up the freight or passengers or receipts, as the case might be, thus reducing or eliminating the benefits from competition. Or, they charged that the railroads cut each other's throat when they competed. The effect of the latter was supposed to be that they charged very low rates for competitive traffic and made up their losses by much higher rates for noncompetitive traffic. Pooling, of course, raised the monopoly bugaboo—that monopoly conditions would prevail generally and that everyone would have to pay what the traffic would bear.

In sum, a picture was drawn that made government regulation of rates and control over service appear necessary if justice were to prevail.

The Facts Were Irrelevant

Theoretically, the charges might be dismissed as irrelevant and immaterial. The railroads were the private property of their owners in almost all cases; as such, the owners should be free to discriminate against whom they would and charge whatever rates suited them and provide such services as pleased them. For good or ill, however, it is this position that is irrelevant. It is historically irrelevant because the railroads have been and are regulated and controlled. It is irrelevant in America because we have a variety of popular government and, if enough of the people can be persuaded that injustice exists, measures will be taken to correct it. In any case, such has happened. Thus, the question of the justice of railroad practices must be tackled head on. This will lead us to an examination of the economics of railroading which will, in turn, clarify the issues which prompted regulation and show why the regulation, when it came, produced the results that it did.

Let it be stipulated, at the outset, that the railroads did sometimes engage in the practices which their critics described. That is, they sometimes charged more for a short haul than a long haul, gave rebates, gave preferential rates to large shippers, favored some shipping points over others, formed pools, gave out free passes, and so forth. Whether such practices worked injustices upon the customers of the railroads is another matter.

To be just means, so far as I can make out, to give to each man his due. In economic terms, it means that a man should have what he has earned or what has been given him by someone who earned it. So long as the railroads provided the service for which they were paid and at the rate agreed upon with each party to a contract, there would appear to be no further question of justice at issue. That is, the practices charged against the railroads could be dismissed simply as involving no instance of violation of contract. If they had, anyone unjustly treated by violation of contract would have recourse to the courts. No new laws were needed to provide such justice.

What the reformers have sought, however, has not been justice. It is sometimes called distributive justice, but it should be called, instead, *equality*. The laws passed restricting the railroads have been animated by the notion that all shippers and passengers of the railroads should be treated equally. They seem to think that each customer of the roads should be charged what it costs to provide the service, plus a "reasonable" profit. To calculate such a charge, it should be necessary only to figure how much it costs to transport a given unit a certain distance and then apportion this among the customers according to the number of units and distance shipped.

Of course, no such calculation can be made. More precisely, if such a calculation were made it would spread disaster in every direction when applied. It could only be an *average* cost per-unit per-distance which would only by sheer luck be the actual cost of shipping one unit a given distance. If such an average cost were then prescribed, it might be expected to bankrupt every railroad in the country not only because the costs of providing rail service vary from one line to another and on the same line but also because they run counter to the whole purpose of the railroad. This is why the government programs have had such a deleterious effect; not because the programs have ever involved so simplistic an approach as the above but because they have worked off modifications of it which ignored the nature of the services railroads perform.

First, it must be made clear who the railroads ultimately serve. Just as in so many other businesses, the railroads serve consumers. Who is the consumer in this case? In the case of goods, the consumer is the person who finally buys and uses them. Though the railroads do serve shippers, they do so only as an auxiliary function to serving the ultimate consumer. In the case of passengers, the consumer is directly the person who is traveling but it would be appropriate to describe those to whom he travels as being, wittingly or unwittingly, the ultimate customers of this service.

In technical terms, what the railroads add is *place* value. In this respect, they are like all other means of transportation. The purpose of transportation is to bring goods and people together and to do so as quickly and inexpensively as possible. Ideally, a transportation system would make available at one's doorstep goods and people from all over the world upon command, in an instant, and without differential charge based on distance transported. As consumers, this is what we desire from transport. A student of the railroads described the service they provide in this way some time ago: "The sole reason why man uses the railway is that it is the most effective agency at his command for the annihilation of space and distance, and it is to be hoped that in the course of time the railway or some other means of transportation will become so efficient as actually to annihilate distance. The one thing that distinguishes the American railway managers from the railway managers of the rest of the world is the success with which they have relieved cities or places of production of disadvantages resulting from their location."[1]

If railroads were to establish rates upon the basis of costs per-unit per-distance, the tendency would be to deny service to consumers which they are set up to provide and to do themselves out of most of their traffic. Producers at more distant points would have to pay more than those nearer by to get their produce to market, and if the distance were great the cost would become prohibitive. This is not what the consumer—that is, all of us—wants. We want as wide a selection of goods and services as possible. The crucial fact is that the railroads can operate effectively only by providing them for us. Hence, the interest of the consumer is identical with that of the railroads. Some local producers, in a shortsighted way, have believed their interests to be at odds with the interests of the railroads—hence, with consumers—and have tried to prevent the railroads from providing transport from distant points inexpensively.

The Economics of Railroading: the Nature of Competition

There are two basic reasons for the identity of interest between the railroad and the ultimate consumer: the particular exigencies of railroading and the nature of competition. Let us examine first the economics of railroading.

Railroads have unusually *high fixed costs,* more, as a rule, than any

---

[1] Meyer, *op. cit.,* p. 361.

other means of transport, and probably as much or more than any other industry. Their fixed costs include such items as laying and maintaining tracks, building and keeping up passenger stations and freight depots, paying for switchyards, rights-of-way, bridges and crossings, rolling

The Library of Congress

The Eads Bridge across the Mississippi at St. Louis, one of the most costly of the early bridges, was completed in 1874. Carriages and railroads traveled on separate levels sixty feet above the water.

stock, safety devices, sidings, and such like. They are unusual, in America at any rate, in that they alone among the means of transport maintain the thoroughfares on which they travel. Wagons, boats, trucks, and planes rarely provide their own thoroughfares; waterways and highways are usually provided at the public expense, though some charge may be made for their use. Railroads usually even own and operate their traffic signals, something unheard of in other large operations. Hence, their costs in preparation for operation are very high.

On the other hand, railroads have unusually *low variable costs* compared with other means of transport. That is, railroads can increase the amount of service provided with declining costs for each additional unit to a point much beyond what is common in other businesses. A train of fifty cars, say, can be hauled for very little more than one of ten cars. Moreover, the cost per mile traveled declines precipitately as the distance is extended, since most of the fixed cost is in loading, unloading, and related activities. To put it another way, given the fixed costs and the fact that a train has been made up, each car added and each mile traveled costs less than the one before it. Railroad practices can be correctly understood only in this context. Railroads have tremendous incentives to increase the length of their trains, the frequency of them, and distance traveled. By so doing, they are enabled to recover their high fixed costs, take advantage of low variable costs, and increase their income. When they operate in this fashion, they are serving the consumer in the optimum manner, for he wants goods brought to him from great distances at low costs.

But, it may be objected, could the railroads not greatly increase their profits by basing their rates on per-unit per-distance traveled? Of course, they could in the abstract; that is, if the volume of freight would remain the same for the higher rates that it would for diminishing rates, they would have every reason to charge those at greater distances proportionally higher rates. The only thing is that the volume would not remain the same, and any railroad management so shortsighted as to suppose that it would, might be expected to bankrupt the company in short order. This brings us to the second reason for the identity of interest between railroad and consumer: competition.

Aspects of Competition

Few things can have been more misunderstood than the nature of the competition with which railroads have been confronted. It is quite common to treat the matter as if competition only existed—prior to automotive and aeronautical transport—when two or more railroads connected with the same points. This is only one kind of competition and in many instances may be less important than others. One writer described the kinds of competition railroads encountered in this way: "competition between carriers by rail, competition with rail and water lines, competition with water lines, competition between markets, or competition of product with product."[2] To which it might be added that passenger traffic is in competition with such other modes of transportation as existed plus alternative uses of money.

Some examples may help to clarify the kinds of competition involved.

---

[2] Henry Fink, *Regulation of Railway Rates on Interstate Freight Traffic* (New York: The Evening Post Job Printing Office, 1905), pp. 9-10.

Any given locale may be in competition with other locales for a particular market. For example, one might consider the market for grapefruit in Baltimore, Maryland. Domestic grapefruit might be brought to Baltimore from Florida, from Texas, or from California. Florida is nearer than Texas to Baltimore, and both are nearer than California. Suppose there were only one railroad from California to Baltimore. It still could not charge whatever price suited it for hauling grapefruit. It would have to meet the rates of rail and ship lines from Florida and Texas. The same would be true, it must be clear, whether there were one or twenty lines from California to Baltimore.

Competing for Markets

The competition for markets is broader and more extensive than the above would indicate. The following is a description of it regarding other products and markets:

> This competition is national and international in scope; not only does the wheat of Dakota compete in Chicago with that of Kansas and Nebraska, but the wheat of the United States competes in Liverpool with that of Canada, Russia, Argentine Republic and India. . . . The Pennsylvania and Virginia coal competes in New England with that from Nova Scotia; the various coal fields in the Alleghenies compete with each other; the Southern iron and Northern iron are competitors. . . .[3]

This competition for market applies even when only one railroad is involved. Distance from the market must be largely negated as a factor in charges for transportation if those farther from the market are to compete with those nearer to the market. For example, if farmers near Poughkeepsie had to pay twice as much as those near Peekskill, if those near Albany four times as much as those from Poughkeepsie, those near Syracuse three times as much as those from Albany, to get milk delivered by railroad to New York City, the chances are good that milk from distant points would never have reached New York City. On the contrary, rates must be approximately the same from all these places to the destination. The railroads want to haul freight, and in order to make distant commodities competitive with those nearby, they will charge less on many occasions than would seem to be warranted by the distance.

---

[3] Charles S. Langsroth, *Railroad Cooperation in the United States* (Philadelphia: University of Pennsylvania, 1899), p. 85.

Competition between products or services must also be taken into consideration. Not only are human wants extensive but also the means for gratifying them are numerous and diverse. The number of foods which, either singly or in combination with a few others, will sustain life and health are so many as to be unnumbered. There are numerous fibers from which to make clothes, a great variety of building materials, a considerable number of fuels, and so on. If the price of any one of these is raised significantly, alternative means are likely to be used to gratify the want. For example, if oranges become more expensive, apples may be substituted. The consumption of commodities for which the demand is elastic will decline as the price rises, particularly if it rises in proportion to the prices of substitutes. This point is appropriate for passenger fares as well as freight rates. Whether one takes a trip, buys some stock, builds a new room on his house, purchases some new contraption, or what not, will be determined in part by relative cost as well as desire. Reduce the cost of travel, and the number of travelers and trips may be expected to increase, other things being equal.

All sorts of economies come into play to check the desire of railroad operators to arbitrarily set charges. It might be supposed, for example, that those within a community served by only one line would be at the mercy of the railroads on incoming freight. It does not follow. "Back-hauling," as it is called, is most important to railroads. The incentive is to haul loaded cars in both directions, and in order to do that, charges must be kept sufficiently low for goods coming in as well as those going out.

The Incentives to Serve

It should be clear from the above exposition, then, that from the nature of railroading and the competition encountered the railroads had great incentive to provide extensive service, reduce the cost of transport, and serve the consumer in the best possible manner for the lowest practical price. By so doing, they would be most likely to recover their fixed costs and to profit from their low variable costs. Any move toward higher charges and the reduction of services would tend to reduce traffic, make it more difficult to meet costs, and work to the disadvantage of the railroads. The historical record tends to substantiate what theory would predict. So long as the railroads were free to do so, they did extend their facilities, improve service, reduce costs, and lower their rates.

Most of the charges against the railroads of discriminating among customers as reasons for regulation are predicated on misconstructions of the nature and purpose of railroading. Of course, railroads did and do discriminate among their customers. One writer put it this way some time ago:

> Discrimination is the underlying principle of all railroad tariffs, whether they have been established by State railroad commissioners, or by the railroads themselves. This is so necessarily. Were it otherwise, railroads could not be successfully operated. Instead of promoting and facilitating commerce, they would hamper and obstruct it, and cause great injury to the public.[4]

Some of the reasons for this should now be easy to see. They discriminated between those distant from the market and those nearer by in order to make the more distant products competitive, between large shipping centers and small intermediate points because of low variable costs, between one product and another depending upon the particular exigencies, between those making large shipments and those making small ones because of various economies involved, and so on.

It was alleged that these discriminatory practices obliged small shippers from small communities not served by competitive lines to pay not only their own way but a part of that of those more favorably located as well. The way to check on this would be to see how much it would cost to provide service to small communities, intermediate points, and those near to market without the other traffic. It would not be difficult to see that in view of the high fixed costs, the low variable costs, and the income from large shipments over a long distance, the railroads would have to charge much more for local service than they did. There is some historical evidence to support this. As government has tried to reduce such discriminations by regulation, the railroads have consistently reduced their local service and discouraged small shipments.

Railroads also discriminated by giving free passes to some people. This practice should be considered as a not very subtle effort at public relations by the railroads which backfired. Free passes were frequently granted to clergymen, newspapermen, politicians, and anyone else in a strategic position to render favorable judgments on them. In effect, the

---

[4] Fink, *op. cit.*, pp. 102-03.

railroads were lobbying to try to prevent punitive action by governments. Not only did the tactic fail but it became another source of discontent with the railroads. In this case, as in so many others, reformers turned the means by which a business attempted to defend itself from government interference into justification for further regulation and control by the government.

Discrimination and Competition

Rebating was a kind of discrimination; but it should be discussed in connection with competition, to which we may now turn for an examination of the charges about it. Why would the railroads give rebates to certain shippers? Why would they not, instead, simply lower the charge? In the absence of government regulation, they could have charged any shipper whatever rate was mutually agreeable.

In the main, what led to rebating before 1887—the year when the Interstate Commerce Act was passed—was the practice known as pooling. Pooling was a device got up by the railroads in a particular area to establish rates between competitive points and to avoid price competition among lines in direct competition with one another. There were two sorts of pools: those in which rates were agreed upon and the traffic divided according to some ratio among the railroads, and those in which receipts were divided among the roads according to some formula. Rebates were means by which railroads secretly competed with one another within a pool, though if the agreement called for a pooling of receipts the incentive to do this was greatly reduced.

Pools were not illegal according to the common law, which in the absence of positive legislation would generally prevail in the United States. The courts would not break them up; neither, however, would they enforce the agreements. Pools had no more standing before the law than, say, did gambling debts. Pools were usually short-lived arrangements, but competing railroads were continually trying to reorganize them after they broke up.

Why did railroad men organize pools? The answer is simple: in order to avoid the requirements of competition. Why did railroad men give rebates and withdraw from pools? The answer again is simple: in order to compete. To resolve this apparent contradiction, yet another facet of competition must be examined along with the historical conditions within which the railroads were operating.

Let Others Compete

There is one side of competition that rarely draws comment. It is this: probably no one likes competition in his own particular undertaking. On the other hand, almost anyone can be convinced of the desirability for others to compete. It is easy enough to understand why this is so. To compete means to offer as good or better services than others, to become and remain efficient, to stay abreast of the competitor's methods and technology, and to lose out when others can do the job better or less expensively. Interest groups usually arise from one of two (or both) reasons: to protect themselves from government, or to get some advantage from government. One of the advantages—the central one—sought from government—is to be relieved of the necessity of competition.

Reformers were not the only ones ambivalent about competition; railroad men were, too. There is a considerable literature in the late nineteenth and early twentieth centuries, some portion of it in sympathy with the railroaders, detailing the "horrors" of competition and calling for government action to abate it. Among the horrors attributed to competition were rebating, rate wars, bankruptcies, and general instability. What many railroad men would have liked would have been for the government to enforce their pooling agreements as contracts, that pools be legalized. Much evidence was gathered which purported to prove that pools did not result in higher rates. Yet, every rebate granted tended to prove the opposite.

Mistaking Symptom for Cause

The facts used to support the claims about the horrors of competition were quite valid. There were rate wars, rebates, bankruptcies, and many railroads in shaky condition. To blame competition for these, however, is to mistake the symptom for the cause. Rate wars are bargain sales or clearance sales; such sales, if they are genuine, are the result of either overproducing or overpricing. It is generally agreed that there was much overbuilding of railroads. The main reason for this was government aid. Several things may have contributed to prices being too high at any given time: pooling, too many roads serving a given area, or inefficiencies of some of the railroads. But one cause may well have led all the others: drastic reductions in the money supply. In such a case—as in the early 1870's and early 1890's—drastic reductions in rates would have to occur in order to continue to keep as much traffic as formerly.

Rate wars, rebates, instabilities, and financial failures were effects not causes. They were effects not of competition but of tamperings with the market, tamperings by governments and the railroads. Competition was the cure, the means by which the adjustments would be made to offset the interferences, adjustments which would mean the triumph of the efficient, the reduction of rates, the consolidation of lines into larger systems, and the providing of the optimum service to the consumer.

Those who proposed government regulation and restriction of the railroads were calling for combating phantom and illusion. They confused effects with causes and cures with disease. They misunderstood the exigencies of railroading and the nature of competition. Their laws reflected this confusion and when put into effect produced the opposite of what should have been wanted.

6 Early Regulation 1887-1920

THERE HAVE BEEN three stages of government regulation of the railroads, though a fourth one appears to be taking shape in recent years. The first stage was that of state efforts at regulation and control, a stage which encompassed such regulation as there was until 1887. In the second stage, 1887-1920, the Federal government began its regulatory intervention and to occupy much of the field. The third stage is bounded by the years 1920-1958, and the Federal government has been the dominant intervener in this period. Since 1958, governments have begun a hesitant shift back toward the much earlier practice of offering subsidies to the railroads.

There have been two different levels of restrictive intervention which cut across the chronological stages. The most obvious level is that of direct governmental intervention by which governments acting by legislation or through commissions have regulated, controlled, restricted, obstructed, prescribed, taken over, aided, or inhibited the railroads in the conduct of their business. The other level is the one on which governments have interfered indirectly by the empowering of labor unions to carry on their activities of extracting agreements from the roads as to working conditions and wages, have aided and subsidized competitive modes of transportation, and have in various ways established surrounding conditions within which railroads operate.

There is no need here to dwell on the first stage of regulation—that by the states before 1887. Suffice it to say that many of the devices and objects of regulation were introduced and tried by the states, such as the establishment of regulatory commissions, prescriptive legislation, rate control, and requirements as to service. The extent of such regulation varied, of course, from state to state and from time to time. Some of the Midwestern states made the most extensive and restrictive efforts. State regulation did not end, either, with the beginning of Federal activity in 1887; certain intrastate rail operations have continued to fall under the states; but, increasingly over the years, the Federal government has preempted more and more of the field.

Federal Intervention and the Crisis of World War I

In any case, the damage done to the railroads by the states was spotty, sporadic, and tended to be localized. Not so, that of the Federal government. The Federal government's intervention intensified from its beginning in 1887 until World War I; the effects reached to virtually all the railroads in the country, and the tendency was to tighten control ever more effectively.

The bitter fruits of this intervention came rather swiftly, and they were such as should have been expected from it. Indeed, attempts to fix rates were less than a decade old when intervention led to a full-fledged crisis. World War I precipitated a crisis for which the intervention had prepared the way. Even before the United States declared war, there was widespread awareness that the railroads were in no position to perform all the services that were expected of them. Exports, mainly to the Allies, in 1915 and 1916 greatly increased the amount of freight traffic. By the time the United States entered the war, government and railroad officials were discussing means and organizing for improvement of rail services. This did not work, and as the months passed in 1917, the situation worsened.

> Poor performances in coal production and distribution led the list of transportation difficulties, although alarm over adequate shipping for food exports and the grain harvest ran a close second. As autumn passed dangerous lows in coal supplies were reported throughout the nation. . . . Between August 12 and November 24 the drop in coal production due to car shortages totaled 20,166,412 tons. . . . By December the possibility of completely empty coal bins faced New England factories and homes. Nor was the coal famine the only major national problem; the annual grain harvest was moving to market slowly because of car shortages and blocked rail facilities.

> . . . Terminal congestion was frightful. Around New York City unloaded freight was actually piled in the space between tracks.[1]

The war exposed the condition of the railroads by placing unusual demands on them, but the war was not the source of the incapabilities of the railroads. The truth was that the United States did not have an integrated rail system: the railroads did not cooperate well with one another; traffic did not flow by the best routes; many railroads were in a state of disrepair; and the routing of boxcars was largely uncoordinated. Despite the fact that historians have long written of transcontinental railroads, there is not to the present day a single transcontinental railroad.

The source of the crisis was the government measures of the preceding three decades. On the one hand, the government attempted to force the railroads to compete; on the other, it refused to allow them to compete. The government proscribed certain kinds of cooperation, attacked efforts at coordination, refused to allow rates to rise in crucial circumstances, and produced conditions in which railroads were considered a relatively poor investment. The thrust of government into railroad regulation had produced an ineffective and disintegrated rail system. To see how this was done, let us turn now to an examination of the regulation.

The Interstate Commerce Act

The first Federal act of regulation was the Interstate Commerce Act, and it was also the basic act from which much of the rest has flowed. This complicated statute, passed in 1887, had many provisions with qualifiers attached to them and the whole was cast in the extensive verbiage and redundancies by which a law is made to close as many loopholes as may be desired. Stripped to their essence, these were its provisions. It was to apply to all interstate freight and passenger traffic by rail. All rates for such traffic should be just and reasonable. Any and all rebates were prohibited. The railroads should not give any unreasonable preference or advantage to any shipper over any other, and should make their services available to all comers on equal terms. A railroad should charge no more for a short haul than a long haul on the

---

[1] K. Austin Kerr, *American Railroad Politics* (Pittsburgh: University of Pittsburgh Press, 1968), pp. 54-55.

same route under substantially similar circumstances, with the proviso that the Interstate Commerce Commission could relieve a railroad from its obligation to conform if circumstances warranted. The pooling (dividing up) of either freight or receipts among competing railroads was prohibited. Rates and fares were to be posted prominently, and not to be changed until public notice had been given. And lastly, it provided for the establishment of an Interstate Commerce Commission to enforce the provisions of the Act.

There were many minor amendments to the Act during the early years, amendments which had the general aim of spelling out and increasing the powers of the Commission. For example: "In 1888 the act was amended to cover classification. . . . In 1889 it was amended to provide for the proper publication of freight and passenger tariffs. . . . In 1889 and 1891 the Interstate Commerce Act has been amended to strengthen the powers of the Commission to compel attendance of witnesses and the production of documents at the hearing of complaints. This provision was further amended in 1895 to protect witnesses from the penal consequences of their own incriminating testimony and to punish recalcitrant witnesses by maximum penalties of $5,000 fine and one year's imprisonment."[2]

Other Restrictive Legislation

The other major acts affecting the railroads before World War I, however, were the Sherman Antitrust Act of 1890, the Elkins Act of 1903, the Hepburn Act of 1906, the Mann-Elkins Act of 1910, the Panama Canal Act of 1912, and the Physical Valuation Act of 1913.

Railroad men generally assumed at the first that the railroads were exempt from the Sherman Act since they already fell under restrictive legislation, but the Supreme Court was soon to rule otherwise. The ostensible purpose of this antitrust legislation was to compel competition. Yet a close examination of it shows that meaningful competition is actually outlawed if the statute were to be literally applied. Section 2 says, in part, that "every person who shall monopolize, or attempt to monopolize, or combine or conspire with any other person or persons, to monopolize any part of the trade or commerce among the several States,

---

[2] Henry H. Haines, *Restrictive Railway Legislation* (New York: Macmillan, 1905), pp. 223, 261.

or with foreign nations, shall be deemed guilty of a misdemeanor. . . ." Certainly a major reason for anyone competing in commercial activities is to gain a larger share of the market. By doing so, he would, in effect, be attempting to monopolize all the trade or commerce in his particular business, though he might not be conscious of so extensive an ambition. Though the statute may not have been applied in just that way, it has been applied to deter growth and expansion and reduce effective competition.

The Elkins Act made it a misdemeanor for railroads to deviate from the published rates, defined unfair discrimination more fully, and provided punishments for officials who might be involved in giving or receiving rebates.

The Hepburn Act was much more extensive; it was comparable to the Interstate Commerce Act as major legislation, and gave the Commission far more power than it formerly had. This Act empowered the Commission to fix maximum rail rates according to the prescription that they should be just and reasonable. The Commission could prescribe uniform systems of accounting for the affected carriers. Moreover, railroads were prohibited from transporting any goods produced by themselves or of companies in which they held an interest except such as would be useful to them in maintaining their roads and related operations.

The Mann-Elkins Act once again extended the jurisdiction and powers of the Interstate Commerce Commission. The provisions for charging no more for a short than a longer haul were greatly tightened. The new act "absolutely forbade lower charges to longer-distance points except after hearing and approval by the Interstate Commerce Commission."[3] The Commission could suspend new rates proposed by the railroads until the court had rendered a decision. The act provided that if a railroad lowered its rates to compete with water traffic, it could not raise them later—after having driven water carriers out of business—until a hearing had been held that would show that some other condition had changed besides the removal of water competitors. A Federal Court of Commerce was set up to hear appeals from the decisions of the Commission, but it was abolished two years later.

---

[3] Frank H. Dixon, *Railroads and Government* (New York: Scribner's, 1922), p. 30.

The Panama Canal Act "provided that after July 1, 1914, it should be unlawful for any railroad to own, lease, operate, or control or have any interest whatsoever through stockholding or community of management, in any water carrier operating through the Panama Canal. Neither was any such relationship to continue elsewhere than through the Canal in cases where the railroad did or might compete with the water line for traffic."[4] This was an attempt to make the railroads compete with steamships.

The Physical Valuation Act was supposed to aid the Commission in setting rates or determining if rates were just and reasonable. The underlying idea was that a rate should ideally be such that an efficient carrier would receive a "fair return" on his investment and that this could somehow be calculated if the value of the property could be ascertained. To that end, the Commission was to make exhaustive computations as to the costs to the railroads of all their properties. The Commission was to "report for each piece of property the original cost to date, the cost of reproduction new, the cost of reproduction less depreciation, and 'other values and elements of value, if any.' " The railroads were "required to aid the Commission by furnishing maps, profiles, contracts, and any other pertinent documents and to cooperate in any way desired in the undertaking."[5] This act is interesting not for any results produced, though the Commission labored many years to try to arrive at the required conclusions, but for what it indicated about the extent to which legislators were willing to go to regulate the railroads.

It should be clear from the above summary of the legislation prior to World War I that the Federal government was gaining more and more control over the railroads and that, conversely, the railroads were more and more circumscribed in what they could do. In addition, labor unions were being given more and more power, but that story will be told in another connection. Something does need to be said about the tendency of court rulings.

The Commission Gains Power

The chances are good that had the Supreme Court been confronted in the 1890's with an Interstate Commerce Commission clearly clothed

---

[4] *Ibid.*, p. 83.

[5] *Ibid.*, pp. 70-71.

with the quasi-legislative-judicial-executive powers which it was later to exercise, it would have declared such a body unconstitutional. At any rate, it is clear from the decisions of the 1890's that the Court considered the Commission to be only an advisory body. Certainly, it did not recognize the Commission as a court; no more could it legislate or execute. But then, neither was such a body in violation of the Constitution. However, the Commission struggled vigorously over the years to have its powers increased, and they were. In the early years, the Court circumscribed the powers of the Commission by ruling on the basis of legislative intent. The Court thus allowed the issue of the constitutionality of such a body to disappear; meanwhile, the legislature made it ever clearer that they intended the Commission to have more and more power. Thus it was that the Federal courts were by World War I largely adjuncts of the Commission in enforcing their rulings.

Undoubtedly, many of those who sought to regulate the railroads in many ways had the best of intentions. They sought to establish just and reasonable rates, extend the benefits of competition to those not receiving it, provide similar services for all shippers, allow the railroads a "fair return" on their investment, and see to it that the general public were beneficiaries of railway services. Good intentions, however, have no discernible effect on results; these are a product of the actions taken. The acts of the regulators were often contradictory, self-defeating, ignored the nature of rail competition, and harmful both to the railroads and the general public. The results were such as should have been expected from such acts.

Even the intent of the regulators as to competition is not clear. On the one hand, they apparently wanted to preserve it; on the other, they wanted to prevent it. One writer describes the aim of part of the legislation in this way: "It attempted to continue competition at points not naturally competitive by the prohibition of traffic agreements, and at the same time to protect other points against such competition by making it unlawful for the railroad companies to discriminate in favor of artificially competitive points."[6] By outlawing rebates, the government attempted to stop that sort of rate competition.

Certainly, one of the ways in which businesses compete with one another is in price. If prices cannot vary from the list price, that sort

---

[6] Haines, *Restrictive Railway Legislation, op. cit.*, p. 326.

of competition is greatly reduced. Another way railroads might compete with one another was in services. But if services had to be extended to all comers on an equal basis, as the law required, a railroad would be greatly hampered in offering better services to a particular shipper than another line would offer him. When a railroad could not work out a more favorable agreement with a connecting line than others could, it was that much more difficult to offer a better price.

The long and short haul clause sometimes made it prohibitive for a weak road to haul commodities long distances at rates competitive with alternative routes. To do so it would have to lower its rates for shorter hauls to a point that would make them unremunerative. A port city, for example, served by financially weak railroads could not expect to compete with ports served by stronger roads. This situation was aggravated by the Panama Canal Act which tended to discourage favorable rail and steamship rates for a particular port. In short, all sorts of competition were hampered by regulation.

As rail regulation became ever more restrictive, it tended to freeze the rail system in its existing pattern. There is every reason to suppose that in the absence of hampering and prohibitive legislation these United States would have had by or before World War I a few great railroad systems spanning the continent in its length and breadth and providing not one but several unified systems of transport. These, in turn, would have been linked with steamship lines to the rest of the world. These several systems would have been in position to compete effectively with one another as, for example, great oil companies do today. Certainly the tendency was toward the linking together and forming of such systems prior to the restrictive legislation.

Financiers in Control

The question is, what froze them into the early pattern? One might suppose that it was antitrust action which prevented or prohibited such unification. Yet antitrust suits did not prevent such expansion and unification before World War I, to my knowledge. Instead, it was the railroad financiers who turned their attention from expanding into new territory and linking together truly transcontinental systems to combining railroads serving the same general area, an effort which has continued to the present day. The most famous early example of this was the formation of the Northern Securities Company. This was a holding company for the controlling stock of the Northern Pacific and Great Northern, two roads serving the same general area. The Supreme Court ordered the holding company dissolved in 1904.

Financiers could and did, however, manage to gain control of railroads serving the same general area by stock purchases. For example, "The traffic of the East and eastern Middle West was dominated by the New York Central and Pennsylvania, allied with the Morgan interests, which controlled the Chesapeake and Ohio, the Baltimore and Ohio, and the Norfolk and Western. Under Morgan's direction, moreover, the New Haven bought control of the Boston and Maine, the trolley lines of New England, and even the Long Island steamship companies."[7] The tendency of such controlling combinations—there were several over the country—was to divide the country into noncompetitive railroad empires, reduce competition within an area, and to delay or prevent integration. If the threat of antitrust action did not prevent such combinations, it is reasonable to suppose it would not have prevented combinations aimed at building integrated transcontinental systems.

Long and Short Haul Rules

We must look elsewhere than the antitrust legislation for an explanation of why financiers did not see any great prospect for profit in building great nationwide systems. It is not necessary to look far, because the long and short haul rules provide a sufficient reason, especially when combined with the rules inhibiting competition. An ideal railroad under the long and short haul clause would be one whose main line connected two or more major shipping centers at considerable distance from one another with only a few intermediate points spaced far apart. In fact, it might be ideal if there were no intermediate stations, for rates could then be set to take full advantage of the economies of operation involved in pulling long trains for very long distances. But a railroad connecting, say, Omaha or Kansas City with Los Angeles or San Francisco might approach the ideal under the long and short haul restriction.

Indeed, there were, and are, several roads well situated to profit from this peculiar regulation. They are such Western roads as the Santa Fe, Southern Pacific, Union Pacific, and Northern Pacific. But there is a counter incentive to linking these roads with those in the East which

---

[7] Arthur S. Link, *American Epoch* (New York: Alfred A. Knopf, 1955), p. 53.

traverse thickly populated areas with numerous intermediate points. This would only serve to tie what had been profitable long haul rates to short haul rates in such a way as either to incur great losses in the short haul business or to price themselves out of much of the long haul traffic. In practice, any Eastern and Western system so linked would be at the mercy of those Western roads free of such ties.

Since the railroads could not effectively compete in so many ways, such opportunity for improving their situation as existed would usually be to combine roads covering the same general area so as to maintain some control over rates and get as much of the profitable business as possible within an area. This is what railroad financiers tended to do. The result, as far as the public was concerned, was a nonintegrated rail system, reduced competition, poorer service, and higher rates.

Other Inhibiting Factors

There were other infelicities produced by regulation. Even where they desired to do so, railroad men were hampered in coordinating services and charges with one another. Not only was pooling prohibited but any other sorts of agreements might make them subject to antitrust suits. It is difficult to imagine an agreement which the officials of two or more railroads might enter into that might not be construed as an attempt to monopolize the transport business of an area. Certainly, if they made any agreement it would likely be with the prospect of increasing business, and any such increase would "tend" toward monopoly.

If rate regulation worked as simply as it has sometimes been conceived, it would have the effect of coddling the inefficient. That is, if by raising rates the income of the railroad could be proportionately increased, and if the Commission wanted to keep every line in operation, the maximum rates would be those which would yield a profit to the most inefficient line. Such rate-setting would have the interesting result of pushing all rates upward insofar as uniform rates prevailed. The Commission has not, of course, behaved in so simplistic a fashion. Even if it did, the demand for rail service is not inelastic. In consequence, rates can be increased without necessarily increasing revenues. The Commission tried to steer a course between raising rates so high that they would reduce traffic appreciably and keeping them so low that many railroads would be ruined. The results were a mixed bag also in the years before World War I: rates did generally rise; some rates were kept too low; many roads were caught in the squeeze of declining revenues.

Statistics indicate that railroad earnings declined after the Interstate Commerce Commission became involved in setting rates. The "aggregate amount paid in dividends fell off $100,000,000 from the high year of this period (1911), and the average rate on dividend-paying stock which was 8.07 per cent in 1908 was 6.75 per cent in 1916. Whatever may be one's personal view as to whether this was or was not a satisfactory financial showing for our railroad system, the fact remained that it did not satisfy the investor. Consequently, the sound policy long practiced by railroad management of keeping ahead of traffic by providing the necessary facilities for handling it was gradually weakened, and at the time the country entered the war the railroad system was far short of that standard of efficiency which the demands of traffic required."[8] One of the signs that the railroads were not spending nearly enough on new equipment was the increase of accidents. Accidents due to derailments increased from 6,697 in 1911 to 22,477 in 1920.[9] In short, government policies reduced earnings, discouraged investment, and set the stage for the railroads to live off past capital investment to the detriment of efficient maintenance.

When World War I came, the railroads were ill-prepared to provide the services wanted. This was, in large measure, due to government policies which had frozen the railroads in an earlier pattern, made it difficult for owners and managers to run them effectively, discouraged investment, supported inefficiency, deterred cooperation and coordination, and inhibited the development of nationwide systems. The Federal government took over the operation of the railroads on December 26, 1917, and continued to run them until 1920. Having prevented an integrated system from developing and thus having set the stage for a crisis, the government took over and did much that it had prevented the railroads from doing.

---

[8] Dixon, *op. cit.*, pp. 23-24.

[9] *Ibid.*, p. 78.

7 In the Grip of Government 1920-1958

If someone had set out with malice aforethought to destroy the effectiveness of the American railroads, he could hardly have devised better ways than those employed by the Federal government for much of the twentieth century—short of hiring wrecking crews to take up the track and dynamiters to blow up the rolling stock. Before World War I, the government subjected the railroads to increasingly debilitating restrictions: by trying to use force to make them compete, not permitting them to compete in many of the usual ways, making it difficult for them to cooperate and coordinate their activities, freezing the systems into their earlier patterns, prohibiting them to follow certain practices by which they could profit and serve consumers, prescribing uneconomic practices, driving investors away, and, perhaps unintentionally, promoting the dissipation of working capital.

Having so circumscribed the railroads as to make it virtually impossible for them to adjust to new demands and changing conditions, the government took over and ran them during World War I. The railroads were technically returned to their owners after the war, but this was done in such a way that the death grip upon them was retained if not actually tightened. While the railroads were bound hand and foot, as it were, government subsidized and promoted alternative means of transport and facilitated the unionization of their employees against them.

Indeed, if railroad managements had been dangerous criminals with lengthy records of dastardly acts, they could hardly have been more carefully watched and had their activities more extensively limited and restrained. In fact, railroad men were treated as second-class businessmen, as charlatans ready at every moment to cheat investors, as extortionists ready to take unfair advantage of customers, as conspirators eager to beset the public, and as brigands on the march to destroy American transport. From another angle, railroaders were treated as if they were truant children whose every activity must henceforth be minutely supervised and whose dealings must be subjected to the most searching scrutiny. In short, men who undertook to operate railroads were, in that capacity, virtual prisoners of their own government.

However, it would be an error to suppose that those directly connected with the operation of the railroads were the primary victims of these government policies. Railroad executives have no doubt generally enjoyed compensation and prestige similar to their counterparts in other industries. Supervisory personnel must have had good salaries over the years. Employees of railroads have usually received relatively high wages. Even stockholders have frequently received dividends and bondholders been paid off. The primary victims of government intervention in the operations of the railroads have been consumers—all of us—who have been denied the best goods at the lowest prices and passenger service of high quality at low prices which they might have otherwise had. It is probably impossible for governments to follow policies that will induce businessmen to serve without compensation, but it is easy to devise policies which result in losses to consumers. This has been the result of the government's regulation of the railroads.

The Socialist Attack

Back of these policies was socialist doctrine, as was indicated in an earlier chapter, however revised and watered down that doctrine might be when it reached the popular mind. More than anyone else, it was socialists who conceived of businessmen as villains preying on the public for private gain. To them, private enterprise was irredeemably flawed by the selfish quest for gain. The railroads received the full brunt of the earliest socialist assault against private enterprise in America. It does not follow, of course, that all who favored regulating the railroads were socialists. Much of the animus for regulation can be accounted for by special interests wishing to use the railroads for their particular advantage. But socialism provided the ideological ammunition—the animosity toward private business, the notion that service should be divorced from profit, and the statist assumptions held by regulators—and the protective coloration for these special interests.

More important, socialism provided a direction and a goal for regulation. The ultimate professed goal of socialists was government control of the railroads and their use for the benefit of the people. Two means to this end have been set forth. One is the government ownership and operation of the railroads. This is the way of what are now sometimes called *doctrinaire* socialists. The other way is more subtle and indirect; it involves government control without ownership and entails a variety of means. This is the way of *pragmatic* socialists. They do not ordinarily refer to themselves as socialists at all in the United States; they prefer to be known as pragmatists, liberals, or some such euphemism. But from the direction of their thrust it can be determined that they are socialists, regardless of the name by which they are known.

Pressure Toward Government Ownership and Operation

Up to and through World War I the pressure of socialists was toward government ownership and operation of the railroads. This was true of several third parties which did not identify themselves as socialists as well as the various avowedly socialist parties. Herbert Croly, a "progressive" socialist, indicated how the goal might be achieved in what he wrote a few years before World War I:

> In the existing condition of economic development and of public opinion, the man who believes in the ultimate necessity of government ownership of railroad road-beds and terminals must be content to wait and to watch. The most that he can do for the present is to use any opening which the course of railroad development affords, for the assertion of his ideas; and if he is right, he will gradually be able to work out, in relation to the economic situation of the railroads, some practical method of realizing the ultimate purpose.[1]

Regulation set the stage for a government takeover by making it increasingly difficult for the railroads to do their job effectively. World War I provided the crisis which was used as the occasion for government operation of the roads. A major propaganda effort was made dur-

---

[1] Herbert Croly, *The Promise of American Life,* Cushing Strout, intro. (New York: Capricorn Books, 1964), p. 377.

ing and immediately after World War I to make the takeover complete and permanent. This campaign did not succeed; it was thwarted by a Congress determined to return the railroads to their owners.

It turned out, however, that only doctrinaire socialism was rejected. American reformism had taken its own peculiar form. Instead of going from operating them to government ownership of the railroads, the government abandoned both of these and turned to full-fledged control. It was sufficient for the day that government have power, authority, and control over the railroads. Progressivism had prepared the way for this direction to be taken. Politically, such a direction is clearly superior to ownership and operation. When government owns and operates, bureaucrats must take on onerous duties and responsibilities; they must provide the services and get the money for operation. Control without ownership provides the bureaucrat with power over but little, if any, responsibility for rendering services. At any rate, this is what was established for the Interstate Commerce Commission in the 1920's.

Regulated Out of Service

It was about as clear as such things can be that when World War I came the government restrictions made it virtually impossible for the railroads to provide the desired services. A railroad historian has recently observed that the "poor condition of the rail lines in 1917 was no doubt partly the result of earlier excessive or mistaken regulation. . . ."[2] Even the Interstate Commerce Commission's recommendations at the time indicated an awareness of the debilitating impact of the restrictions. The Commission recommended that the government either take over and operate the railroads "or that all legal obstacles to the complete unification of the railways for that period be removed. . . ."[3]

Once in power over them, the government reversed its former policies toward the railroads. What was sauce for the private enterprise goose definitely was not sauce for the government gander. William G. McAdoo, who was placed in charge of the railroads, proceeded to do all sorts of things that had been either prohibited or beyond the power of rail executives. Rail service was speedily coordinated; the railroads were

---

[2] John F. Stover, *The Life and Decline of the American Railroad* (New York: Oxford University Press, 1970), p. 175.

[3] Sidney L. Miller, *Inland Transportation* (New York: McGraw-Hill, 1933), p. 156.

treated as if they were a single system. Freight was routed the shortest way. The government discriminated vigorously among shippers, giving war goods preference. Passenger service for the general public was greatly curtailed. The railroads had for several years been denied any significant rate increase. "Under the Federal Control Act it was unnecessary to secure the approval of either state or federal regulatory bodies for changes in rates. . . ." New rates could simply be proclaimed: thus, "the Administration announced, on May 25, 1918, a 25 per cent increase in freight rates effective a month later. . . ."[4] Of course, the government was free also of antitrust restrictions and could and did treat the railroads as a giant trust.

Even so, the railroads were in bad shape when they were returned to their owners in 1920. McAdoo and his successor had seen fit to accumulate a huge deficit rather than raise rates sufficiently to cover costs. "The official report of the Railroad Administration admitted that the total operating expenses (plus rentals paid to the individual railroad companies) exceeded total revenues for the twenty-six months of federal operation . . . by just over $900,000,000."[5] And this figure does not include more than $200 million later paid to the railroads for undermaintenance during the war. This latter figure, however, amounted to only about one-third of what the railroads claimed they were due for undermaintenance. The railroad owners were stuck with an inheritance of high wages to employees, excess equipment constructed for wartime purposes, and roads that had generally been run down.

The Transportation Act of 1920

Had the management of the railroads been left free to operate them as they saw fit, they might have been able to revive the roads. They were not. Instead, they were much more completely shackled than ever by the Transportation Act of 1920. This act should be considered the crowning piece and culmination of Progressive legislation. The agitation of the Progressives produced antitrust activity, a spate of legislation, several constitutional amendments, and heady intervention in foreign affairs. By the end of World War I, or before, it appeared to have lost its impetus. Americans were weary of reform and were registering their

---

[4] *Ibid.*, p. 163.

[5] Stover, *The Life and Decline of the American Railroad*, *op. cit.*, p. 173.

feelings at the polls. Even so, one more piece of Progressive legislation was pushed through, one which was typical of what Theodore Roosevelt had advocated as the Bull Moose candidate in 1912—that the government leave property ownership in private hands but subject the great industries to stiff regulation. Of course, Roosevelt supposed that the railroads were already so regulated, but the principle which he would have applied to all industry was carried to its logical conclusion in the Esch-Cummins Transportation Act.

Much early policy was reversed. The Interstate Commerce Act had prohibited pooling. The Transportation Act of 1920 authorized the Interstate Commerce Commission to approve pools if it could be shown that they were in the public interest. Antitrust legislation had been aimed at one corporation indirectly controlling others. The new act authorized the Commission, "upon application by any carrier or carriers and after hearing, to approve 'the acquisition . . . by one of such carriers of the control of any other such carrier or carriers, either under a lease or by the purchase of stock or in any other manner not involving the consolidation of such carriers into a single system for ownership and operation,' upon such a basis as may be found by that body to be just and reasonable."[6]

Planned Consolidation

The Act charged the Commission with the task of preparing and adopting "a plan for the consolidation of the railway properties of the continental United States into a limited number of systems. In the division of such railways into such systems under such plan, competition shall be preserved as fully as possible and wherever practicable the existing routes and channels of trade and commerce shall be maintained. . . ." To make it possible for this to be accomplished, the act permitted the Commission to authorize consolidations of railroads into single corporations according to the master plan.[7] Actually, the Commission has never put any such plan into effect. They are waiting, no doubt, until mathematicians square the circle before undertaking so forbidding a task as this.

No longer was it legal for anyone to build or extend a railroad at will.

---

[6] Miller, *op. cit.*, p. 175.

[7] All such authorized actions were specifically exempted from antitrust suits.

The act required that a prospective builder must first have a "certificate of convenience and necessity" from the Commission before beginning construction. Moreover, the law provides that "no carrier . . . shall abandon all or any portion of a line of railroad or the operation thereof unless and until there shall first have been obtained from the Commission a certificate that the present or future public convenience and necessity permit of such abandonment."

The restrictions on railroad finance were equally restrictive. Following a brief period of grace after the act went into effect, "no securities might be issued legally by any carrier subject to regulation except upon Commission approval."[8] The act lays down the general principles upon which such approval may be granted. It notes that Commission approval does not in any way imply that the United States government guarantees such securities. The only securities a railroad might issue without Commission approval would be notes maturing within two years and even such borrowing was restricted to 5 per cent of the par value of outstanding securities.

Rate Control

The most amazing provisions of the Transportation Act of 1920, however, were probably those having to do with rates. The Commission was authorized to fix rates for roads under its authority according to how it grouped them from time to time. The rates were to be fixed so as to assure a fair return upon investment if the railroad were efficiently run. Initially, Congress declared that a fair return in most instances would be 5½ per cent annually of the aggregate value of railway properties. Any railroad that earned more than 6 per cent on the aggregate value of its properties in a given year was to have one-half of the excess placed in a reserve fund for its own future use and the other one-half to be turned over to the Commission to place in a general contingency fund to aid ailing railroads. What was involved was a most complex limitation on earnings and a redistribution plan.

There were several other rate provisions of the act. The Interstate Commerce Commission was granted virtual pre-emptive authority over rates so far as state regulatory bodies were concerned. If it found that state regulations occasioned any prejudice or inconvenience to inter-

---

[8] Miller, *op. cit.*, p. 177.

state commerce it could negate them. For the first time, also, the Commission was empowered to prescribe minimum as well as maximum rates. It could also prescribe the division of joint rates between or among two or more carriers if it found the prevailing division to be unjust. The long and short haul clause was altered so as to further limit the exemptions the Commission could grant from its provisions.

Routing and Service

The Commission was granted extensive powers over routing and service. A carrier found "improperly" diverting traffic from another line would be liable to the extent of paying the whole amount gained to the "injured" railroad. The Commission was authorized to divert traffic to other lines if, in its opinion, a road was unable to provide a service. Moreover, the Commission was empowered to determine what routes interchanged traffic should take. Should car shortages develop, the Commission could direct their disposition so as to relieve the difficulty without regard to the desires of the owners. The law provided that it should be the duty of every carrier "to furnish safe and adequate car service and to establish, observe, and enforce just and reasonable rules, regulations, and practices with respect to car service." Nor was the Commission to be particularly concerned about private ownership of terminals and surrounding trackage. If the Commission should find that it would be in the "public interest," "it shall have the power to require the joint or common use of terminals, including mainline track or tracks for a reasonable distance outside of those terminals. . . ."[9] The owners were to be paid something for such usage, of course.

Certain of these provisions have been altered over the years. The Emergency Railroad Transportation Act of 1933 attempted once again to effect consolidations of lines into larger and more stable systems. The attempt to prescribe earnings precisely had already been more or less abandoned. The Transportation Act of 1940 placed restrictions on competitive modes of transportation. But the government grip upon the railroads by way of the Interstate Commerce Commission has generally remained. That hold was authorized and established by the Transportation Act of 1920, and its provisions amply illustrate the extent of the grasp.

---

[9] *Ibid.*, p. 182.

A state of organized irresponsibility was established by this legislation. The power to make managerial decisions of wide and determining scope was vested in the Interstate Commerce Commission. The responsibility for operating the railroads remained with private management. But that management was denied the authority to make on its own all sorts of decisions by which entrepreneurs ordinarily operate businesses efficiently and successfully. Rail executives could not, and cannot, buy, sell, build, abandon, or dispose of their facilities without Commission approval. They could not sell stock to raise new funds nor consolidate with other lines without the authorization of the ruling government body. In most of the usual ways, railroad managers could not compete with rail or other modes of transportation, could not compete in price, in supplying of certain kinds of service, or even, if the Commission so ruled, in the exclusive use of better located facilities.

No Room to Operate

Critics of railroad management have long claimed that those running the roads were cautious, unimaginative, disinclined to innovate, and lacking in vision. In view of the limitations under which they operate it would hardly be surprising if the charges were, in substance, true. Any new service innovation could be quite expensive to the railroad. It might not pay off, yet the road might be stuck with providing it indefinitely because the Commission decided that the "public interest" required it.

The crucial factor in explaining the "unimaginativeness" of rail management, however, is the tying of rate structures to earnings. When this is combined with government engendered inflation—that is, increase of the money supply—as it usually has been since 1920, it is easy to understand why managements have been reluctant to make daring innovations. Increases in money supply mean that prices in general must rise to offset the increase. Yet railroads have to observe a time lag before they can raise their prices, if it turns out that they are permitted to do so. To get the raise, they need to demonstrate that their earnings are insufficient under the present rate structure. The effect of this is that railroads can rarely expect to turn a good profit by extending services, but they can lose a great deal. In short, railroads cannot—under inflationary conditions—make much of a profit; they can, however, have horrendous losses.

Actually, however, rail executives have often been quite imaginative.

They have even made interesting service and equipment innovations from time to time, but that is not what I want to point out here. Much of the managerial imagination has not been expended in finding ways to improve and expand service, as it normally would be. It has, instead, been devoted to finding ways for a railroad to survive and make a modest profit under the crushing burden of restrictions, to finding ways to circumvent the thrust of regulation, and to finding arguments and evidence to convince the Commission to permit some course of action.

Holding Against Disaster

Railroad men have fought a fifty-year-long holding action against disaster. Denied most of the avenues by which they might advance, they have husbanded their resources by strategic retreats. They have developed ingenious arguments supported by voluminous arbitrarily construed statistics for reducing services—for dropping passenger trains, for cutting off dining cars, for closing depots, for not installing warning systems, and so on. They have become, in effect, *un*businessmen, for rather than seeking to expand services, they have sought to reduce them; rather than increasing traffic, they have sometimes sought to reduce it; rather than reduce prices to increase the number of customers, they have often sought to raise prices and have thereby reduced customers and revenue.

These unbusinesslike actions make sense only in the framework of restrictions that has been erected. The reversal of priorities from expanding services through innovation to reducing services can be explained, and the explanation will show that it was about as good business as could be done. Denied much expectation of profits by new exertions, railroad men turned to making what profits they could by as little effort as possible. They sought to keep only that business which was most profitable, involved the least risky outlay of funds, and entailed the least amount of effort to acquire and service. They sought to use the rails where they were most clearly superior to other modes of transportation and to avoid competition where superiority was less certain.

Under such policies, the railroads ceased to be a growth industry. Indeed, they appear to be an industry dying of a lingering illness. One after another they have abandoned or had taken from them services that they once performed: the carrying of mails, the hauling of most packaged freight, much of the passenger service, and so on. Each time a railroad lops off or reduces service to an area it is apt to reduce the number of customers for even its profitable traffic. For example, when passenger service to a small community is discontinued, it reduces the likelihood that people traveling at however great distances will go by train when either their point of departure or destination is that city. Cut off enough such service and even long distance trains between great cities will not have enough passengers to warrant the provision of the service. The same principle will generally hold regarding any such service, and the railroad policies have undoubtedly produced the appearance of a dying industry. These policies, in turn, have been the result of desperate measures taken by railroad men caught in a stranglehold by the Interstate Commerce Commission.

Had this been all, the railroads might still have held their own. But there was more. They were faced by increasing competition from other modes of transportation. And while they were being circumscribed by onerous restrictions, governments were frequently aiding and abetting their competitors. That part of the story needs also to be told.

8 The Grip of Privileged Competitors

As LATE as World War I, the railroads were king of American transport. Virtually all of the intercity freight within the United States moved by rails. For practical purposes, there were no competitors for passenger transport, if steam and electric lines were both properly considered as rail transportation. So great was the preponderance of the railroads that governments had come to treat them as the only effective means for moving either people or goods to most places within the country. In the parlance of politicians and reformers, they had a monopoly of transport. Judging by the Transportation Act of 1920, Congress expected this preponderance to last indefinitely into the future.

It was not to be, of course. Looking back from the perspective of a half a century, it is now clear that the railroads had reached and passed the peak of their dominance of transport by the time that law was passed. The total railroad mileage in the United States had already begun to decline. It reached a peak of 254,037 in 1916 and had dropped slightly to 252,845 in 1920. This downward trend has continued over the years. By 1930, it was down to 249,052; by 1940, 233,670; by 1950, 223,779; by 1960, 217,552; and by 1968, it had fallen to 209,000.[1]

Of themselves, the figures for total railroad mileage might signify little. But when combined with the statistics for passenger and freight traffic they help to illustrate the declining condition of the railroads. The most drastic decline has been in passenger traffic. It is estimated that in 1926

[1] John F. Stover, *The Life and Decline of the American Railroad, op. cit.*, p. 155.

the railroads provided 39.5 billions of passenger miles of transport for people. There was an absolute decline in this over the years; the figure was 28.6 billions in 1956.[2] In 1968 there were only slightly over 13 billion passenger miles by rail. Relative to the total passenger miles by every means of intercity transport the rail total declined much more drastically. The rail share of such transport by all common carriers was estimated to be over 83 per cent in 1926. By 1956 it was only a little over 35 per cent. When private transport was taken into the estimate, the rail percentage for 1926 was 22.48. By 1956 it was only 4.09.[3] "In 1968 the slightly over 13 billion passenger miles of rail travel were only a half of the volume of bus travel, and less than one-seventh of the total air carrier traffic. The rail traffic constituted less than one-tenth of the total commercial intercity traffic, and was under 1.4 per cent of the total private automobile travel."[4] As things have been going, the passenger train will soon join the oxcart in the museum of abandoned transport.

More Freight—Less Revenue

The freight tonnage hauled by the railroads for distance has not generally declined over the years. In 1926 the railroads carried a little over 452 billions of revenue ton-miles of freight. In 1956—a good year for rail freight—the total was over 655 billions of revenue ton-miles. But the rail share of this intercity traffic has declined greatly over the years. It was estimated to be 76.56 in 1926, and to have fallen to 48.22 in 1956.[5] However, the percentage of revenue coming to the railroads *vis à vis* that to other modes has declined much more than the percentage of freight ton-miles might lead one to suppose. For example, "the rail share of combined truck-rail freight revenues fell from 67.4 per cent in 1940 to 38.7 per cent in 1955.[6]

What has happened most generally is that the railroads have made their gains for the most part in low-rated bulky commodities and lost much of the high-rated traffic, which accounts for the relatively greater

[2] There was a tremendous increase of passenger traffic during World War II. It declined precipitately after the end of the war, though for several years it was still above the prewar level.

[3] Nelson, *op. cit.*, p. 18.

[4] Stover, *op. cit.*, p. 193.

[5] Nelson, *op. cit.*, p. 10.

[6] *Ibid.*, p. 27.

decline in proportion of revenues received than of freight ton-miles transported. Certain kinds of traffic have been taken away from the railroads almost entirely. In 1922 there were 80,000 railroad stock cars; the number had declined to 20,000 in 1966. "Long-haul furniture vans soon made boxcar movement of household furnishings a thing of the past, and the increased use of intercity trucking caused a reduction of less-than-car-load lot freight from 51,000,000 tons in 1919 to 1,000,000 tons in 1966."[7]

It has been commonly supposed that these absolute and relative declines in passenger and freight services by the railroads were an inevitable consequence of the development of other means of transportation. Undoubtedly, automobiles, trucks, buses, barges, pipelines, and airplanes have, each in their own way, advantages over rail transport. Automotive transport on highways has much greater flexibility than that on rails. Water transport is much less expensive. Air is much faster. The public might well welcome and use these alternative means of getting goods and people to distant places.

However, we do not know with certainty today which of these is superior to others in transport in many ways and which the consumer would prefer for what in the open market. This is so because governments have intervened so extensively in transport that the market for transport has been greatly distorted. Almost all of this intervention in the twentieth century has been detrimental to rail transport and much of it has been advantageous to other means of moving goods and people. The restrictive legislation on the railroads has already been surveyed. Here, the task is to examine government aid to other means of transport and the much less extensive and later regulation that generally has been the case there.

What happened to the railroads in relation to other means of transport can be put succinctly. The railroads were regulated, restricted, restrained, and circumscribed: their rates were set, expansion and contraction limited, investments monitored, competition hindered, and services prescribed. They were bound hand and foot, as it were, most managerial leeway taken from them, vested with responsibilities without corresponding freedom, and treated as though their owners and managers were irresponsible children. Their would-be competitors, on the other hand,

---

[7] Stover, *op. cit.*, p. 128.

were given special privileges, were fostered, succored, developed, and were for varying periods of time little hampered by restrictive legislation.

Subsidized Highways

Much of rail traffic has been diverted to the highways. People in ever larger numbers have turned to travel by way of the private automobile, and buses and taxis have provided transport for those not having or wishing to use their own conveyances. Trucks have come to haul larger and larger portions of intercity freight as well as that within cities. New governments have long played some role in road building, maintenance, and, of course, such policing as was done. From the 1830's—when the Federal government abandoned extensive projects and state governments shifted their activities elsewhere—to the 1890's most road building was done by local governments, frequently counties. States began at about that time to play a larger role in road construction. They were doing much more by World War I, by which time automobiles and trucks were in widespread use.

The Federal government began to evince an interest in highways once again in the 1890's. Initially, this interest only resulted in such activities as surveys. To this end, $2,997 was spent in 1894. However, Federal expenditures grew over the years until by 1916 $662,785 was spent. In the latter year, the Federal government went more directly into highway construction by authorizing grants-in-aid to states "to establish post roads, regulate commerce, provide for common defense and promote general welfare." It entered much more extensively into road building by way of the Federal Highway Act of 1921. According to that Act the Secretary of Agriculture was to designate a system of interstate highways. For the construction of roads so denominated states were to be granted half the cost on a matching basis. Road building then got underway in earnest. Total expenditures for roads by all levels of government increased from approximately 1⅓ billions of dollars in 1921 to 2½ billions in 1930. The Federal share of spending increased from 4.68 per cent in 1921 to 37.11 in 1938, after which it decreased somewhat for a number of years.[8] Total government expenditures for road construction

[8] See Marvin L. Fair and Ernest W. Williams, *Economics of Transportation* (New York: Harper, 1950), pp. 68-69.

rose rapidly once again in the 1950's; by 1957 it had reached $5,662,000,000.[9] The Federal percentage began to increase once again also. This was even more the case as the Federal government gave priority to the Interstate system and began to fund it vigorously after 1956.

Railbeds Are Taxed

That the development and use of the highways had a debilitating impact on the railroads is clear. It should be clear, also, that governments were promoting highway use by road building and maintenance. The power of eminent domain was brought into use to acquire routes. The power of taxation was used to finance construction and maintenance. Governments undertook the erection of safety devices, patrolling, and the provision of auxiliary services such as aid to motorists in distress. They were aiding one form of transportation while they were restricting and inhibiting another. Whether those who have used these roads have borne the full burden of the costs is an interesting question, though one difficult to answer. Much of the cost has been paid by user taxes, such as those on gasoline, oil, tires, and so forth, but by no means all. It has been estimated that between 1921 and 1965 a total of $216 billions were spent by all governments within the United States on roads and highways. Only about 60 per cent of this has come from user taxes, leaving some $80 billion to be made up elsewhere. One writer notes that "a considerable fraction of the $80 billion of tax money clearly has provided a *public* route for the more than 16,000,000 buses and trucks which crowd our highways today."[10]

There have been efforts in recent years to close the gap and to have the users of the roads and highways pay for them fully by way of taxes related to their use. Even when and if this is done there is the much debated question of whether trucks and buses are paying their share through the taxes. This last question can be left for the experts to hassle over, but there is one difference between the users of the highways (and the users of airways and waterways) and the railroads that incontestably favors the former. The railroads have generally been treated as private property and have thus been assessed heavy real property taxes by local governments over the years. By contrast, highways are generally

---

[9] Nelson, *op. cit.*, p. 76.
[10] Stover, *op. cit.*, p. 137.

Union Pacific Railroad Photo

Trailer-on-flatcar train on Cajon Pass, California.

governmentally owned and are free from all property taxes. The result is a subtle but real promotion of highway use *vis à vis* the railroads by government. There are other differences to be taken up below.

Waterways

If there is doubt about the extent of government subsidization of highway travel, there can be little about the amount and extent of that of the use of the waterways. One writer notes that total "federal appropriations for the rivers and harbors program amounted to $4.6 billion through fiscal 1954. It has involved improvement and maintenance of some 286 commercial seacoast harbors, 131 Great Lakes harbors, and 22,500 miles of waterways, including several multiple-purpose dams."[11] Extensive expenditures have been authorized more recently for the St. Lawrence Seaway and the Ohio River, among others. States and cities have also undertaken improvements of ports and waterways. For exam-

[11] Nelson, *op. cit.,* p. 85.

ple, the state of New York widened and deepened the Erie Canal early in the twentieth century at an expense of $176 million.[12] In consequence of all these expenditures there has been a dramatic rise in freight ton-miles shipped over water.

Users of the waterways pay little, if any, of the expense of improving and maintaining the rivers and harbors. Such costs as these users have, one economist notes, are "only the expenses of owning and operating equipment and of rendering services. Nothing is included for operating, maintaining and amortizing the federal investment in waterways . . . or for tax contributions on public waterway facilities."[13]

Air Travel

Air travel has also been extensively subsidized by governments. Most of the major airports in the United States have been built and are maintained by local governments, or agencies set up by them. The Federal government has also made extensive grants for the establishment of airports. Weather information for take-offs, landings, and flights is provided by the Federal government. Air space over the United States is, in effect, owned by the Federal government, and authority over it is exercised by the Federal Aviation Agency. Acts passed in 1926 and 1938, according to a summary, authorize and direct "the Administrator of Civil Aeronautics to designate such civil airways as may be required in the public interest, and authorizes him to develop, establish, improve, operate, and maintain air navigation facilities wherever necessary. . . ."[14] Between 1925 and 1957 something over one billion dollars was spent in this operation within the United States. Airlines were rather extensively subsidized, at least in the early years, by government contracts for carrying the mails. A study made of the situation for 1940 concluded that if all subsidies to commercial airlines had been eliminated for that year, "gross revenues would have fallen from the actual $65,000,000 to only $50,550,000 and operating expense would have increased by $8,000,000. The 1940 net income of $6,900,000 would have been converted to a deficit of $15,300,000."[15]

Airplanes have not been quite as fortunate as barges and ships in the

---

[12] Fair and Williams, *op. cit.*, p. 90.

[13] Nelson, *op. cit.*, p. 90.

[14] Quoted in *ibid.*, p. 94.

[15] Fair and Williams, *op. cit.*, p. 114.

use of these governmentally provided facilities. They do have to pay for some of the facilities and services, at least some portion of the cost of them. Airplanes pay a fee to land at airports. They also pay a tax on fuel which partially pays for services rendered. However, there can be no doubt that the airlines have been heavily subsidized by governments. The House Committee on Appropriations observed in 1954: "This committee has year after year called attention to the fact that the Federal Government is providing huge sums for airway facilities and operations without reimbursement from the aviation industry. The committee does not propose to continue indefinitely making . . . such large appropriations unless some system of airway user charges is placed in effect. . . ."[16] Nonetheless, Congress has in recent years turned to the development of commercial aircraft.

It may be objected that the railroads were aided also in the early period of development. So far as it goes, the statement is correct, but there are some significant differences between that and the aid given to competitors in more recent times. In the first place, no new aid was given to the railroads by the Federal government (until very recently) after 1871; nor, so far as I know, was any extensive state or local aid given after that date. In the second place, the Federal aid was repaid over the years. That which was extended as loans was, in general, repaid with interest. The lands granted were paid for over many years by the individual railroads which hauled government cargoes at reduced rates. One writer describes the culmination of the latter in this way: "Land-grant rate reductions and voluntary equilization of rates by competing railroads up to June 30, 1943, totaled an estimated $580 million. Since this was several times the value of the land grants at the time land was granted for railways and it exceeded the sums derived by the railroads from the grants, the Congress in 1945 relieved land-grant roads of the obligation and land-grant reductions ceased as of Oct. 1, 1946."[17] As for state and local aid, it has probably been repaid many times over by property taxes.

Other Aids to Rail Competitors

Governments have not only hamstrung the railroads with regulation, restricted them in various ways, taxed them, and subsidized competitors,

[16] Quoted in Nelson, *op. cit.*, p. 99.

[17] *Ibid.*, p. 69.

but they have given benefits of other kinds to other forms of transport. They were usually regulated much later. Motor carriers did not come under general Federal regulation until 1935. They have also protected competitors rather assiduously.

The Federal government has been most solicitous in the protection of water transport. It has frequently taken care to see that railroads did not underprice and drive out water carriers. A fantastic example of this solicitousness occurred several years ago when the Southern Railway proposed to haul grain in huge boxcars at greatly reduced rates. This, it was supposed, would have considerable effect on the transport of grain by barges on the Tennessee River. Therefore, the Interstate Commerce Commission held lengthy and involved hearings, going from town to town in the Tennessee Valley to explore the ramifications of the matter. In like manner, the railroads were long prohibited from the use of the "unit train" as a means of lowering rates. Bus and truck rates have usually been lower than rail rates. It is likely that this frequently would not have been the case were all means of transport competing vigorouly and freely with one another.

Franchise Privileges

Newer modes of transport have not only been subsidized and protected but also given special privileges. The most notable of these special privileges is the franchise. All interstate trucking common carriers have franchises for their activities. In like manner, states frequently license and franchise intrastate and intracity carriers. Entry into the taxicab business is usually restricted in some similar fashion. In like manner, airlines have their routes granted to them, and a limited number are permitted to service any area.

It may be objected that the railroads were also franchised. So they were, but this had a somewhat different rationale. Railroads were expected to provide their thoroughfares, safety equipment, and stations—all of which were or became quite expensive. Franchises and other aids were granted to lure entrepreneurs into the business. By contrast, airlines, trucking, and water transport companies have not provided their thoroughfares, rarely provide safety equipment except that on their conveyances, and frequently do not provide their stations. Certainly, franchises were not needed to lure men into the trucking business, and it is doubtful whether airlines were for long promoted by this privilege. In any case, trucking and airline franchises were different; they were and are special privileges to use facilities provided by governments. The highways may have been built initially for all to use, but only those with special charters may use them commercially as common carriers. In like manner, the airways are there; they are open space above the earth altered only by surveillance and the provision of take-off and landing facilities. Yet, only a most limited number of companies are permitted to use them for scheduled commercial purposes.

These chartered privileges have usually been granted in such ways as to protect established businesses and assure, so far as possible, the prosperity of those engaged in them. By limiting entry, governments have endeavored to see that only those would offer service who could continue to provide it, that they were protected from numerous small competitors, and that those earliest in the field would not be unceremoniously shoved out. If the railroads ever had such protection, it has long since lost its earlier significance. In any case, the railroads have long been stuck with special responsibilities while their competitors have been granted special advantages.

This work should not be mistaken, however, as a brief for the railroads. If it is a brief for anyone, it is a brief for the consumer. And the consumer has frequently been disadvantaged by government policies on all means of transport. The limiting of entry to various fields has reduced the price and service competition which the consumer would otherwise have enjoyed. In interstate moves of household furniture today, for example, the shipper pays tribute, wittingly or not, to some company which has the good fortune to be franchised. The moving company involved may not own a single piece of moving equipment—though some of them do—nor have any of its employees touch one item of household goods. Whether it does or not, it gets a considerable cut out of the moving bill because it holds a franchise for the interstate movement of household goods to the appropriate places. Whether it performs a commensurate service can be determined by doing away with all such franchises and seeing how well such companies fare.

Less Restraint on Private Noncommercial Transport

Yet another major infelicity has resulted from government intervention in commercial transport. However late it has come, regulation and restriction has come to almost all commercial transport in greater or lesser degrees. By contrast, private noncommercial transport has much fewer and more limited restrictions and restraints. For example, one may operate his personal automobile without a special franchise, may travel by whatever route of highways he chooses, have as his destination whatever town in whatever state he pleases, notify no authorities of his intention, abandon any service he has provided to others, cease to travel regularly between points where he customarily did, sell his automobile if he grows weary of it, and so on through an extensive list of freedoms. So may he do with his truck generally, so long as he does not haul for others. With some reservations, much the same can be said for private airplanes and boats, and for railroads that go nowhere of commercial interest.

The consequences of this difference between the government treatment of commercial and private transport are everywhere to be seen. It is most apparent on the highways and city streets but it can also be seen in the airways and waterways. Much of public transport has been abandoned, shifted from the railroads to highways, or is in varying degrees of trouble. City street transportation systems have become money losers in numerous places. By contrast, private conveyances proliferate: they clog the highways and streets, are now said to menace the airways, and make many waterways hazardous. Not all of this should be attributed to differential government intervention but much of it should. Hampered common carriers and largely unhampered private carriers result in inordinate growth of private conveyances and stultification of common carrier enterprises.

The railroads are, however, the main subject of this work, and it is appropriate to focus upon them once again. They have been throttled by regulation and restriction, had their traffic reduced by aids given to competitors, and been made to look as if theirs was a dying industry by special protections to competitors. They were also the earliest major industry to have large numbers of their employees organized in labor unions. That part of the story must now be told.

9 The Grip of the Unions

Government throttled the railroads in three ways mainly. In the first place, restrictive regulation took away crucial managerial authority from the railroads and vested it in the Interstate Commerce Commission. This was supplemented, in turn, by various legislative inhibitions of general application. In the second place, government subsidized and otherwise privileged competitive means of transport. In the third place, government fostered the organization of railway unions and aided them in various ways in circumscribing and hamstringing the use of rail facilities. The first two of these interventions have already been covered. It is time now to examine the grip of the labor unions on the railroads.

Labor unions, in general, are organized to get higher wages and improve the working conditions of their members. To do this, they attempt to take the determination of these conditions out of the market place and have them determined by negotiation with the employer who negotiates under the threat that he will be denied access to any workers if he does not comply with their demands. The economic impact of this intervention extends outward to effect with varying degrees four distinct groupings of people.

Those who are apt to be most directly affected by labor union activity are other potential workers for an employer. They are most likely to be the ones against whom threats and violence are used if there is a strike—and if the employer attempts to operate the struck facility. Other workers are the ones, also, who are denied the opportunity for jobs which they might have if unions did not prevent them from being employed. More broadly, if unions succeed in getting higher wages and better conditions than they would otherwise have got, they do so by reducing the number who can be employed in that undertaking, as a rule. The general impact is either to reduce the number who can be employed or reduce the wages and working conditions of some of those employed, or both.

Less directly, labor union activity is aimed at employers (though union rhetoric suggests that they are the primary target). Employers are not usually the victims of threats and violence, but this does not mean that they may not suffer. They may and do suffer during a strike by sabotage, by additional charges incurred in attempting to protect and maintain facilities, by having to go to the trouble and expense of training new employees, or by being unable to operate their facilities and provide goods and services with all the train of disadvantages that may follow from that.

Labor union activity may, in the third instance, have effects which reach through to all of us as consumers. This is so, obviously, when a prolonged strike cuts off goods and services which we could otherwise have had. It is so, too, when labor costs are raised so that goods and services are made more expensive. In this case, the consumer may shift to substitutes or reduce his consumption of the goods or services involved.

The fourth effect is rarely, if ever, discussed and has not, to my knowledge, had any careful empirical studies made which would tend to verify it. Yet it is an effect which can be reasonably adduced and which much evidence that is common knowledge tends to support. The effect I have in mind is on those who work in and use the facilities of employers whose employees are extensively organized into unions. Those facilities are likely to show the effects of the tampering with the market which produces an imbalance in capital outlay. If an employer has to pay higher wages for shorter hours, if his workers attain various perquisites which hamper their use, if he must still compete with others in providing the goods and services, if he must compete for money with other users, then something has to give if he is to operate successfully. That something will quite often be the appearance, style, and quality of his facilities.

I noted in an earlier chapter that railroad facilities are frequently rundown, that freight and passenger stations are often decrepit and in poor state of repair, that passenger cars are old and dirty, and that facilities in general are below the standard in other fields. Railroads have obviously skimped in expenses for facilities in order to meet other outlays. This, in turn, has had a rather predictable effect on employee morale, and helps to account for surly and desultory service. In one direction, at least, the union quest for better working conditions has resulted in worsening working conditions.

Growth of Railway Unions

The railway unions were among the earliest trade unions organized on any scale within the United States. The Brotherhood of Locomotive Engineers was organized in 1863. The remainder of the Big Four of the Brotherhoods were organized within the next twenty years. In addition, two other major union developments occurred in the nineteenth century involving railway employees. The Knights of Labor gained considerable following among them, and even brought off a successful strike against the Gould System in 1884-85. In the 1890's, Eugene Debs organized the American Railway Union which brought off, temporarily, a sympathy strike for Pullman workers. However, the Knights of Labor and the American Railway Union were short-lived organizations, while the Brotherhoods had much greater permanency.

Union membership grew in the early twentieth century and had a great surge during World War I after the government took over the railroads. Since that time, the unions have remained strong and, though they have rarely struck, it is generally conceded that they could shut down the railroads rather effectively if and when they did. Many of the unions have remained independent, but some of them are affiliated with the American Federation of Labor or with the Teamsters.

The Government and the Unions

The relationship between the government and the railway unions needs to be made clear at this point. To do this is no easy task. Not only has the nature of this relationship usually been mired in controversy involving the legitimacy of union activities but also the relationship itself has been complex and confusing. Presidents, governors, and government officials have frequently attempted either to be or appear to be neutral in the contests between unions and railroad companies. They could not be, though this fact has frequently been kept from public attention. They could not be, most basically, because union tactics would not permit them to be. Government must be either for or against labor unions as they have been constituted and operated. There is no middle ground.

The reason for this can be made clear by a little examination into the nature of labor unions. According to union rhetoric, labor is not a commodity. The import of this is that wages should not be determined in the market but should be determined elsewhere. Again, according to the rhetoric, wages should be set as a result of negotiation. Not, however, by negotiation between the employer and the individual employee; according to widely held notions, that became impracticable due to the development of large companies and corporations.

The notion that wages are, or ever have been, determined to any significant degree by negotiations is a red herring used to throw the inquirer off the scent. It is true that occasionally negotiations may occur between a prospective employer and someone who has a much needed skill, ability, or reputation, and when the prospective employee has several prospects. But this is the exception to the rule by which wages are determined. There is usually a going wage in the market at any given time for a particular job, a wage rate resulting from competition among employers for workers and among workers for jobs—that is, from the supply of workers and the demand for their produce. Any negotiations that would occur would be on the fringes of the question of wages and working conditions.

Can a Union Negotiate?

How, then, could a union induce an employer to negotiate with its leaders for workers? To put it another way, if a company could hire workers at a wage its managers were willing to pay, why would those managers negotiate the matter with labor union leaders? The answer, it is clear both in theory and in history, is that they would not do so willingly. This means that for the union to be brought in, some compelling reason must exist.

In order to be able to negotiate as an equal with an employer, a union must corner the market of workers available to him. This can be done in one of two ways when the task is stripped to its essentials. A union might, in theory, corner the market by placing available workers under contract to it and paying them the wages and providing the working conditions it demanded from any other employer. This would be a market operation, and the union would be going into the market to bid for workers. Negotiations could then take place between prospective employers and the union for workers by negotiating to buy the contracts. In fact, no such operation has ever been undertaken by a union, nor is it likely to be. Unless a union had unlimited funds employers need only hold out for a time to bankrupt and break the union.

Unions do attempt to corner the market, but they do not use market methods to do so. They attempt to deny the employer access to workers and the constructive use of his facilities until he comes to terms. They do this, if he attempts to operate, by intimidation—by strikes, by driving prospective employees away from the facilities, by sabotage, and by threats. They have no recognizable good or service to sell; they have no workers under a work contract for a period of time which could be transferred to an employer. All they have to offer is an agreement to refrain from their tactics of intimidation for a period of time in return for certain wage scales and working conditions to prevail for those who work for an employer.

Government cannot, I say, be neutral toward the use of such tactics. It must either prohibit and inhibit intimidation or it must condone it. It must either enforce contracts arrived at by coercion or it must negate them. Government must either monopolize the use of intimidation or concur in the use of it by others. There is no middle ground.

Railway unions posed the dilemma very early in their operations for government of whether to side with or against them. They posed it more dramatically than most unions have done. They did so because of the nature and importance of the railroads. Trains are particularly vulnerable to the saboteur. A twisted rail, an incapacitated engineer, a rail wrongly set to take a train into a siding, strategically greased rails, can cause an amazing amount of mischief. Moreover, a station or switchyard shutdown can prevent the effective use of the extended facilities of a railroad. On the other hand, large portions of a wheat crop could be lost by the denial of rail service at a crucial time, and large cities would be hard put to survive. In consequence, those who governed have been confronted with the dilemma of either preventing the use of intimidation by unions or throwing the weight of government behind the unions so that rail companies will be forced to make sufficient concessions or comply with what is wanted and thus make the unions' tactics unnecessary. In short, they have had to use force either on the companies or on the unions.

Government Sides with the Unions

Government—both Federal and state—took the side of the unions, at first tentatively, and then over the years much more thoroughly. They have done so in three ways, mainly. First, the Federal government threw its weight behind the mediation of disputes. This favored the unions because in the absence of intimidation there is no reason to suppose the companies would have wished to resort to mediation to settle disputes. (Of course, given the threat of intimidation, the companies might, and did sometimes, want mediation more than the unions did.) Second, both Federal and state governments prescribed such things as hours of work, compensation for overtime, and various sorts of work rules. Third, by supporting negotiated agreements, by requiring companies to adhere to them, and by other tacit aids governments encouraged the growth of unions.

The first national labor law of any sort was the Act of 1888 which was concerned exclusively with the railroads and the unions. It was the first tentative step toward government support for arbitration of disputes. This Act provided that if the parties to a dispute chose to do so they could submit it to a Board of Arbitration which would have the power to subpoena witnesses and get testimony. Compliance with the decision of the Board was to be voluntary. The Act also provided for a Presidential Commission to be appointed upon request, a commission which would be authorized to publicize its findings.[1]

This first Act was hardly used; in consequence, it was supplanted by the Erdman Act in 1898. This Act provided that once the dispute had been submitted for arbitration and a decision made, the decision was to be binding on both parties. The Erdman Act also contained rules which supported labor union organization. "It was made a misdemeanor for an employer to require the execution of an oral or written yellow dog contract from any employee as a condition of employment, to threaten or discriminate against any employee because of union membership...,"[2] and so forth. This part of the Act, however, was shortly nullified by the Supreme Court, but it does indicate how far toward the support of unionism Congress was willing to go at this date. The Newlands Act

---

[1] See Philip Ross, *The Government as a Source of Union Power* (Providence: Brown University Press, 1965), p. 19.

[2] *Ibid.*, p. 21.

passed in 1913 strengthened the mediation features of the Erdman Act.

Around World War I, the Federal government began to prescribe the length of work day for rail employees, or, more specifically, the terms of payment for time worked. "In 1916, under threat of an imminent railroad strike, Congress within four days passed the Adamson Act, giving trainmen the 'basic' eight-hour day without wage reduction. Overtime payment at 'time and one-half' was required for railroad workers in 1919."[3]

The Federal government took over and operated the railroads during World War I. The policy toward organized labor during that period, and its results, is described by one work in this way: "During federal control of the railways from 1917 to 1920, public policy encouraged organization by forbidding antiunion discrimination and by introducing nationwide agreements on hours, wages, and working conditions. . . . Like organized labor at large, the railway brotherhoods made great strides during the war years."[4] Also, the government devised a whole series of job classifications which tended to rigidify the role of a given worker; in addition, seniority rules were set up and enforced.[5]

The Transportation Act of 1920

The Transportation Act of 1920 included extensive provisions that were supposed to lead to settlement of labor disputes. It declared that it was the duty of representatives of management and labor to arrive at a settlement. If they failed, the matter was then to go before a Labor Board. The Board was supposed to decide "all disputes with respect to the wages or salaries of employees . . ." not settled by negotiation. Not much came of this, however, because the unions wanted to deal with disputes nationally—that is, treat all railroads as belonging to a single system—while the companies insisted upon separate negotiations for each system.

New methods were set up in the Railway Labor Act of 1926. "It places primary emphasis on direct collective bargaining and mediation, but also establishes voluntary arbitration and compulsory investigation." This Act was amended in 1934 by an act which established a

[3] Merle Fainsod, *et al., Government and the American Economy* (New York: Norton, 1959, 3rd ed.), pp. 163-64.

[4] *Ibid.,* p. 184.

[5] Ross, *op. cit.,* pp. 29-30.

National Railroad Adjustment Board. By this latter act, also, labor unions were effectively empowered by government. "The 1934 amendments to the Railway Labor Act forbid company unions. The roads must negotiate in good faith with the authorized labor representatives certified by the Board, although agreement is, of course, not compelled. Carriers may not engage in a number of specified labor practices, such as promotion of company unions, yellow-dog contracts, and other hindrances to independent unions."[6]

The tendency of the Federal government's special protection of railroad workers is also indicated by the Emergency Railroad Transportation Act passed in 1933. The Act authorized mergers and consolidations of rail facilities to be overseen by a Federal Coordinator. But workers were to be protected as follows:

> The number of employees in the service of a carrier shall not be reduced by reason of any action taken pursuant to the authority of this title below the number as shown by the pay rolls of employees in service during the month of May, 1933 . . . but not more in any one year than 5 per centum . . . ; nor shall any employee in such service be deprived of employment such as he had during said month of May or be in a worse position with respect to his compensation for such employment, by reason of any action taken pursuant to the authority conferred by this title.[7]

The above are examples rather than a full-fledged account of the way the Federal government aided in fastening the incubus of unionism on the railroads. Part of the effort was motivated by the desire to avoid ruinous strikes, but all of it has been undertaken with a politician's eye to the vote of privileged union men. The railroads were the first to receive such government attention. The laws governing railroads, unions, and negotiations between them have been special acts. Other unions generally fall under general acts. The effects of this special status of railroad unions have been with us longer than the effects of the general legislation. The government has, on the one hand, empowered the unions to act as a monopoly; on the other, it has attempted to restrain them

---

[6] Fainsod, *op. cit.*, pp. 185-86.

[7] Henry S. Commager, *Documents of American History* (New York: Appleton-Century-Crofts, 1963), p. 271.

from taking full advantage of the position. The railroads have been caught between the Scylla of monopoly unions and the Charybdis of continual government intervention in negotiations.

States have also passed legislation along lines sought by unions. An example of this is the full-crew laws passed by a number of states. New York State passed such a law in 1913. The situation in 1960 was this:

> In its present form, New York's full crew law specifies a minimum number of operating employees on freight trains of more than twenty-five cars, on freights of fewer than twenty-five cars, on passenger trains of more than five cars, on light engines, on fuel-electric engines and on locomotives used in switching operations.
>
> For the most part, the minimum crew specified is larger than crews required by existing contracts between the railroads and employe organizations. Thus trains entering New York from other states are frequently required to stop at border points to pick up extra crewmen.[8]

Other such rules have to do with distance to be traveled by a workman, and such like. Where states have not prescribed crew sizes, they are usually provided for in union contracts.

Stultifying Effects of Government Action

The economic effects of union action empowered by government and of government action supported by unions have been burdensome and stultifying on the railroads. They have hampered the use of personnel in economic ways by the railroads, have concentrated workmen in the least productive undertakings, have denied the railroads the benefits of technology, have fastened antique practices on the roads in perpetuity, and have contributed much to the decline of the railroads and to over-all railroad employment. Some examples will show how this has been done.

Railroads are hampered by rigid work rules in the employment of their personnel. For example, "Where yard service has been maintained road crews may not perform switching for their train, even though no yard crew is on duty at the time. Such a yard crew must be called to do the work; otherwise the road crew may claim an extra day's pay at

---

[8] Leo Egan, "Rail Crews and Politics," *The New York Times,* (January 28, 1960), p. 35.

the yard rate for a few minutes' work in switching, and the yard crew not called may similarly claim payment." Again, "On some roads a road crew may not double over in taking a train from a yard. Transfer crews may set cars on an industrial siding, but they may not spot them for loading or unloading. A switching crew must be brought up to do that. In most yards switching crews must be called at set hours. If called later, penalty payments accrue. Hence locomotives and crews, called at stated hours, stand idle until business flows in some time later, but during the same trick."[9]

Rail Labor Costs Excessive

Railroad costs for labor have frequently been proportionately higher than other modes of transportation, that is, have accounted for a higher proportion of operating costs. "In 1939 the percentage of pay-roll costs, with taxes and depreciation included in operating costs, was calculated for various types of transportation as follows:

Class I line-haul railways	53.8
Air transportation	40.7
Water carriers	39.0
Motor truck transportation	38.2
Motorbus transportation	35.2
Pipe-line transportation	31.7"[10]

There are several reasons for these higher costs. One is that railroad workmen frequently work much less than an 8-hour day to get credit for one or before overtime begins. One book estimates that the average crew under average conditions in the freight service could complete its work day in 6¼ hours and that a passenger crew could do so in 4⅓ hours.[11] Such work rules obviously drive the cost of labor upward.

An observer seeing a freight train pulling 125 cars on a long distance haul with only a few crewmen aboard might suppose that railroads were making money hand over fist. After all, this looks as if it would be a much more economical use of personnel than could be matched by any other means of transportation than perhaps barges or pipelines. But such an observer would only be seeing that part of railroad operations

[9] Fair and Williams, *op. cit.*, pp. 626-67.

[10] *Ibid.*, p. 607.

[11] *Ibid.*, p. 625.

that keeps them going despite all else. In point of fact, a considerable portion of the labor costs of railroads is concentrated in the least productive and least remunerative operations. They are employed on freight locals where several men may handle only a few boxcars in the course of a day, on switching and siding operations, on passenger trains, in small stations which do little to no business but maintain an agent and sometimes other personnel, on commuter trains which operate only at certain hours, and so on.

When railroads introduce labor-saving technology they are frequently prevented from reducing labor costs significantly. Labor unions may not oppose the introduction of new equipment, but they do oppose the laying off of workmen, the shifting of them to less remunerative employments, or the reduction of work crews.

Some sorts of services have undoubtedly been priced out of the market by work rules. For example, "The height of absurdity in full crewing appears to have been reached upon a medium-sized railroad when a modified small auto delivery unit was placed on flanged wheels to perform passenger service on a branch line. When a crew of five men was required to man it, its utility for the purpose disappeared and the service was abandoned."[12] I used to wonder why railroads did not widely use one-car self-propelled units to carry passengers on branch lines. They could bring long-distance travelers to and from main line stations as well as provide service from villages and small towns to cities. The reason is now clear. Despite the fact that one man operating such a unit would not have as much to attend to as a city bus driver, the unions would insist that several men be employed in the undertaking.

Decline in Service

The grip of the unions on the railroads has produced a train of results of most doubtful desirability. This grip has contributed to the decline of passenger and freight service, to the removal of the railroads as competitors in the providing of many kinds of services and to certain areas, to the decline of railroad employees, to the cost to the consumer of his use of rail service, to the deterioration of morale of both employees and consumers, and to the decrepit state of many of the rail facilities.

---

[12] *Ibid.*, p. 627.

There may be those who suppose that it was enlightened policy for government to maintain an uneasy peace in railroading by empowering unions, by fostering negotiation, and by substituting the intimidation of government for that of unions on occasion. There may be those who suppose that government established monopolies are desirable if the objects sought are in accord with their wishes. Yet it is proper to ask whether those who think in this fashion believe that it was desirable so to hamper, constrain, and limit the railroads that they could no longer effectively offer many of their services and could no longer attract customers in some areas. If this latter was not desirable then the former could not be enlightened either. The grip of the unions, the grip of government regulators, and the grip of privileged competitors—all under the auspices of government power—have combined to reduce the railroads to their present debilitated state.

10 The Future of the Railroads

VIRTUALLY everyone who has any interest in and knowledge of the transportation situation in the United States must agree that the railroads are in trouble and that their difficulties are very closely related to a host of other transport problems.

The vast Penn Central system is bankrupt. One after another once famous passenger trains have been cut, and less well known ones have since been canceled. Most companies say that they lose money on their commuter business. Street transportation companies in most cities are generally money losers. Traffic congestion is endemic around and within most cities of any size. Exhaust from the internal combustion engine used on automobiles, buses, and trucks principally is a major pollutant of the atmosphere. Railroad unions are perennially on the verge of striking and tying up transportation throughout the length and breadth of the country. Highway building in the urbanized areas of the country goes on at a torrid pace and yet it always appears to be behind the rising demand for highways and streets. Disposal of waste—in some considerable part a transportation problem—is a mounting burden.

The decline of the railroads is not a development isolated from everything else in America; the effects extend outward to the much more comprehensive matter of all of transportation, and what happens to transportation affects the commercial and fraternal life of a people.

Proposals for doing something about the transportation situation have not been wanting. Governments at various levels have begun tentative and hesitant reversals of long term policy toward the railroads within the last decade or so. Politicians have at long last ceased to talk of the railroads as if they were a menace that somehow has to be contained else it will destroy the country. They have begun to treat them more as if they were respected elderly grandparents, for whom some provision must be made in the period of their dotage. Subsidies are now being provided for various commuter trains and some for longer distance ones. The Federal government is about to commit itself to take over and run the remaining passenger trains, if the companies cannot do so. In a similar fashion, cities have been subsidizing or otherwise taking over street transportation systems.

Proposed Remedies

One proposal which has much support is that government should devote itself to coordinating the various modes of transportation within the country as well as the international carriers under its authority. Indeed, Congress charged the Interstate Commerce Commission with some such task as this for surface transportation in an act passed in 1940. The preamble said:

> It is hereby declared to be the national transportation policy of the Congress to provide for fair and impartial regulation of all modes of transportation subject to the provisions of this Act, so administered as to recognize and preserve the inherent advantages of each; to promote safe, adequate, economical, and efficient service and foster sound economic conditions in transportation and among the several carriers; to encourage the establishment and maintenance of reasonable charges for transportation services, without unjust discrimination, undue preferences or advantages, or unfair or destructive competitive practices; to cooperate with the several States and the duly authorized officials thereof; and to encourage fair wages and equitable working conditions; all to the end of developing, coordinating, and preserving a national transportation system by water, highway, and rail, as well as other means, adequate to meet the needs of the commerce of the United States, of the Postal Service, and of the national defense.[1]

All this may sound quite plausible on paper. Why, indeed, should the government not develop a national coordinated system of transportation? Why could it not use the carrot and the stick, alternating with regulations

---

[1] Quoted in Fair and Williams, *op. cit.,* pp. 727-28.

and inducements skillfully administered so as to achieve this national goal?

The most direct reason why government cannot develop a coordinated transportation system is in the nature of politics. Politicians operate by conciliation and compromise. They attempt to balance interest against interest, region against region, rural population against urban, and so on. Whichever interests are at the moment most clamorous and crucial to election victories will receive the most attention. It is difficult to see how this would be likely to result in coordinated economic activity.

At a little deeper level, it can be seen why government would not succeed in this even if it could mirror the electorate much better than it usually does. Government intervention tends to fix relationships in patterns that have existed at some time in the past. This is so, not only because government action inhibits change and places obstacles in the way of adjustments to new circumstances, but also because any sort of factual basis upon which men would operate to coordinate transportation would be taken from the past—i.e., would be historical. If all the data that might conceivably be brought to bear on transportation were fed into a computer, the answers that could be obtained from the computer, so far as they would be factual, would be answers for some time in the past. To make the point concrete, it might be possible to construct a model for a coordinated transportation system for 1925 on the basis of data now available. But none can be constructed now for 1975 except by extending current figures—that is, fixing it in the present pattern—or by speculating as to what will be needed in the future.

The Uncertain Future

The deepest reason why government cannot intervene so as to provide a coordinated system is that no one knows what modes of transportation are wanted in what quantity and of which quality in the future. The present writer does not know how many passenger trains between which points may be wanted in the future. He does not know whether there should be more or less than there are at the moment. He does not know how many hopper or grain cars will be needed next season, how many automobile carriers, how many gondolas, how many flat cars, where a new railroad should be laid and an old one discontinued, where new stations should be built and old ones abandoned, and so on. This writer does not know, nor does anyone else, what will be wanted in the future. If he did know, he could become fabulously rich by providing it at just the right time and right place. But alas, such infallible foresight is denied to us mortals, whether we are clothed with the powers of government or not.

This being the case, a coordinated transportation system, if there is to be one, will have to be built by trial and error, by speculation; and it will never be completed until all change has ceased. This means that there will be malinvestment, that there will be waste, that some of the speculations will not pay off. This is one of the central arguments for having such speculations made by private investors rather than government. If government agents guess wrong, we all pay. If private investors guess wrong, they lose.

But we do not all simply pay once and get it over with if those in government guess wrong about what is wanted; we may continue to pay and pay. Politicians do not readily give up when they are wrong; they frequently continue to throw our good money after their bad decision. They have fertile imaginations when it comes to thinking of reasons for operating enterprises at a loss. If they operate passenger trains which have only an occasional passenger, they can still justify it on the grounds that if an all-out war came the trains would still be needed, along with many other reasons of like character.

Past experience indicates, also, that if government enterprises do not succeed economically, the politicians rather than blaming themselves will blame the people, or, more precisely, some portion of the people which can serve as a scapegoat. Government power may then be used to make the people fit the Procrustean bed of facilities that government has provided. It is easy to see how this might work with a coordinated transportation system. The more popular modes could be scheduled at inconvenient hours and the less popular ones at peak hours of transport need. Increasing restrictions on the use of private automobiles and trucks and airplanes would likely be made in efforts to make governmental facilities pay off. (Of course, private companies like to have such aids as these from governments when they can get them.)

Summation of Evidence

But it is not necessary to resort to the imagination to examine the effects of intervention. This work has already explored many of these in detail in connection with the railroads. The main reason there is not now a coordinated system of transportation in this country is government intervention. A summation of the conclusions from evidence already presented will make the point. Government intervention in railroad activity has:

1. discouraged investment by limiting earnings and prescribing conditions of operation.

2. discouraged innovation not only by harassing investors but also by making railroads continue costly operations once they have been established.

3. discouraged consolidations that would have produced truly transcontinental systems by the long and short haul clause as well as other devices.

4. discouraged competition by establishing rates and service requirements and by fostering consolidations among naturally competitive lines.

5. subsidized and advanced other modes of transportation while inhibiting railroad competition by regulatory measures.

6. empowered railroad employees against the companies by supporting unionization, by sponsoring collective bargaining, by establishing seniority systems and work rules, and by fixing an expensive retirement system on the railroads.

7. produced bankruptcies, coddled inefficiency, and adopted penalties of one kind or another for the efficient.

8. fostered overconstruction at the outset, prevented the abandonment of unremunerative lines and facilities, and required the railroads to pay for expensive safety measures which are usually provided at taxpayer expense for other modes of transportation.

9. taken from railroad managements most of the authority for making entrepreneurial decisions but fastened upon them the responsibility for continued operation.

The list could surely be extended but the point emerges:

The present transportation mess is a result of government intervention. The railroads have been greatly limited in their appointed task of helping to link the country together commercially and fraternally. They have been hampered, restricted, limited, inhibited, harassed, regulated, pushed, pulled, and controlled. The fact that some railroads can still operate profitably is testimony to the great economic advantages of this mode of transportation.

The Federal government is now proposing to take over and operate passenger trains if the companies will not continue them. Already subsidies are being provided for the Metroliners on the Penn Central and for some commuter trains. There is a familiar pattern in this activity. Governments first adopt restrictions and regulations which inhibit private enterprise in providing certain services. Then, they enter the field to provide the services. It has happened with city transportation systems. It has happened with housing. Once in the field, governments extend their domain, and taxpayers are called upon to make up the losses incurred by government operation. What community in America will not want a Metroliner? And what politician will not see votes in requiring the government to provide it?

Some railroads may see a bonanza in all this. But they should long since have learned to beware of governments bearing gifts. It is easy to see that if government operates passenger trains, and private companies the freight trains, a contest will quickly develop over which shall bear what proportion of the costs. Government can bankrupt line after line by shifting the costs toward freight, thus setting the stage for government takeover of the railroads.

Free the Market

There is a way out of this mess, however, which promises much better results. It is a way that even the railroads may be too timid (or too fearful) to suggest. It is a way that promises much for investors, for management, for workers, and, above all, for consumers. It is the way of freedom rather than control. It is the way of economy rather than waste. It is the way of service rather than servitude. It is the way of mustering the ideas and abilities of numerous men rather than the stultifying concentration of decision-making power which now obtains. It is the way of prosperity rather than depression, of life rather than death for an industry.

In short, turn the railroads loose! Remove the restrictions, limitations, controls, prescriptions, and regulations which now hamper and restrain them. Allow them to serve in whatever ways they can and will, profitably and felicitously. There is no reason why they should not be allowed to, and every reason why they should.

Union Pacific Railroad Photo

Aerial view of Bailey Yard, North Platte, Nebraska.

If what is wanted by Americans is a coordinated transportation system which will provide for their transportation needs, then one of the ways they can hope to have it provided is to turn the railroads loose, turn them loose to charge market determined prices, turn them loose to form whatever combinations may appear to those involved to be desirable, turn them loose to extend services where they will and to abandon those that are unwanted, turn them loose so that their managements can make the entrepreneurial decisions, turn them loose to hire whom they will at whatever wages are mutually agreeable between employer and employee, turn them loose from the grip of subsidized and privileged competitors, turn them loose to take advantage of their low variable costs and allow them to increase their proportion of the traffic so as to meet their high fixed costs—in short, turn them loose from the ubiquitous grip of government.

The most direct way to accomplish this would be to repeal the vast century-long tangle of state and Federal legislation affecting the railroads. Abolish the Interstate Commerce Commission and the various state regulatory commissions. Remove all prescriptions as to rates, service, investment, sale, abandonment, long and short hauls, new construction, and so on. This would leave the railroads free to manage their own affairs. Remove all the special privileges extended to labor unions. Cease to subsidize competitors in various ways.

Chaos Now Prevails

Americans have been taught to believe over the years that chaos would result if this were done. It is true that we could expect many changes if railroads were freed from restrictive and inhibiting legislation. One of the things that might be expected is that under the prod of economic necessity railroad men would begin to shake off their lethargy and become more vigorous. Competition would revive: among railroads, with barges, with trucks, with automobiles, with airlines, and so on. Railroad managers might be expected to cease thinking of ways to curtail service and to start thinking of ways to extend it. As some railroads began to be quite profitable, investors would be lured into putting more money in them. Stocks whose prices have been stagnant for decades might be expected to begin to fluctuate considerably. Imaginative entrepreneurs would dream of nationwide rail systems and move to form them. Prices of rail services would fluctuate, differ from company to company and region to region. New sources of goods and services would be opened up to vie with established ones. Some services would be abandoned and new ones would be conceived. Truckers, barge lines, and airlines would feel the spur of competition. Companies that could not compete successfully would sell out or go out of business.

If this be chaos, it has never been clear why the consumer should fear it. It is clear why all sorts of vested interests might and do fear competition and enterprise, why those in the business fear competition for they may not be able to hold their own, why labor union leaders and those with seniority fear the competition of would-be workers, and why truckers, barge lines, and airlines would fear freed railroads. But the worst the consumer—which is all of us—has to fear from competition is lower prices and better service. If the increase of choices and decisions he is offered be chaos, then many would no doubt welcome such chaos.

Actually, we have the chaos now, the chaotic tangle of legislation within which all commercial transport operates, the chaotic patchwork of railroads over which goods and people must pass to go from coast to coast, the chaotic situation on the streets and highways as vehicles of a vast assortment of shapes, sizes, and operating conditions vie with one another for limited space, a chaotic situation which results in the rending crashes which produce their annual huge tolls of dead and wounded bodies and vehicle destruction, the imminent potential chaos which strikes perpetually threaten, the chaotic structures and facilities of a declining railroad industry unable to attract new capital, and so on. It is ironic to fear that freedom would result in chaos when we are confronted on every hand with chaos, both actual and potential, much of which has resulted from intervention.

Of course, the railroads are not the only means of transport that should be freed. Others are restricted and restrained by regulation also. It is this restraint of commercial transport, while leaving individual transport free, which has produced so much that is unwanted today, so many of the deaths and injuries on the highways, so much of the congestion, so much of the pollution, and so much of the contest for limited space. If we continue to inhibit commercial transport, we shall, no doubt, have to place increasing restrictions on individual transport. There is another way. It is to free all transport of any restraints that are not directly related to protecting life, liberty, and property. Coordination will occur within the marketplace; professionals will do much of the work of transport; the amount of congestion and pollution will probably be greatly reduced; and the choices of means and quality of transport will increase. Such a prognosis is warranted from past experience with the market.

As things stand, the future of the railroads is bleak. So is the future of consumers of their services. Over a period of about ninety years, virtually every sort of intervention has been tried—intervention which has brought us to the present pass. It is time for yet another experiment—an experiment with freedom.

11 | Epilogue: The Impact of Intervention

GOVERNMENT INTERVENTION in railroading has had a devastating impact over the years. A vital industry has been transformed by it into a declining industry. Many services once performed are no longer performed or poorly provided. Competition has greatly declined, costs have risen, profits have usually been low, and labor trouble is endemic. What has gone before shows clearly the relationship of government intervention to all sorts of untoward developments in railroading.

If government intervention had elsewhere been attended with great success and had failed signally only in its effects on the railroads, we might be warranted in concluding that it had failed only because of inept and unintelligent application. The United States government appears to be operating on some such assumption as this presently. The government is beginning to shift from its long term policy of restriction toward subsidization. Actually, those who offer apologies for such shifts in policy would not be likely to admit that the earlier intervention was inept and unintelligent. Their apology would be a little more complex. They would announce that times have changed, and that new conditions call for new solutions. The assumption would be that subsidies in the early years of railroading were justified, that later regulation and restriction was necessary, and that now new subsidies are warranted. We can be reasonably sure that this would be the line because the arguments for relief from taxes, removal of restrictions, and the making of loans or the provision of other sorts of subsidies are frequently made on the basis that older practices are outmoded.

The argument from changing circumstances begs the question. The question is whether earlier intervention worked as it was supposed to. If it did not, as has been shown to be the case with the railroads, why did it not? Was it because of the ineptitude of the intervention? Or was it because government intervention, by its very nature, produces such consequences? The effects of intervention elsewhere offer a partial answer to the question.

The debilitating effects of intervention on the railroads is not an isolated instance of such effects. My own studies and reading have confirmed for me that it is generally the case. Sometimes, the effects of intervention are so direct in producing the opposite of what was wanted that they are readily apparent. Such has been the case with the New Deal farm programs and the later extensions of them. These programs were supposed to aid the small farmer and to reverse the flow of population from the farms into the cities. The results have been just the opposite: the benefits have gone, in the main, to large farmers, and the flow of population into the cities was accelerated.

Some Results Are Obvious

The impact of some interventions have clear and predictable results. For example, the establishment of price controls with the maximum price below what the market price would be results in shortages. Contrariwise, the support of prices above what the market price would be results in surpluses. When wages are thus supported, there is a surplus of labor, i.e., unemployment. The increase of the money supply, other things remaining equal, will result in higher prices. These and other such economic principles can easily be illustrated with a hundred historical examples.

Some interventions have results that branch off in a variety of directions, some results being fairly obvious, others more or less obscure. Such have been the consequences of government intervention on behalf of labor unions. The most obvious results are increased unionization, effective strikes, the tying up of industries, higher wages and prices. There are many other less obvious results: the pricing of some products out of the market, the pricing of some workmen out of the market (unemployment), the arraying of workmen against workmen in strikes, the political pressures of labor unions for government programs that will reduce the available labor supply, and so on.

Some interventions even appear to have salutary results because so many of their effects are hidden from view. This has frequently been the case with government's increase of the money supply (monetary inflation). Much that is attractive follows from this activity. Prices rise; debts contracted earlier can more readily be paid; money is much more plentiful, and a sense of economic well-being may be widespread among the populace. Investments of ready capital expand industries and offer higher levels of employment. The consequences follow in ways that are not usually readily identifiable with the cause. A contraction of the money supply—something that was bound to occur in the fairly short run so long as the monetary expansion had occurred by way of an increase of bank deposits when banks both operated on fractional reserve and men could demand gold for their currency—reverses the above effects and produces what is called a depression. If the money supply is not contracted, the eventual result will be an inflationary level that will make money, and all things expressed in it, worthless. But there are numerous intermediate effects of inflation. Inflation discourages saving, because money loses value as it is held. Those who have already saved will have the value of that saving dwindle away. Contracts expressed in monetary terms are only partially fulfilled.

An Endless Chain of Interventions

Government regulation restricts, confines, diverts, focuses, makes inflexible, and alters the course of men's actions in hundreds of ways. Government programs are almost invariably predicated on the notion that a single cause will have a single and predictable effect. If prices rise, the answer to this, simplistically, is price controls. But it is not. For there are then shortages of whatever is controlled. Producers turn their production into uncontrolled areas. Energies are diverted into a hundred channels to evade the restraint. Government regulation can be likened to an attempt to dam a river on a vast and extensive plain. Build a dam athwart the path of the river and it will overflow its banks and follow new courses, perhaps many where there was once one. A series of new dams will only be followed by the same results, multiplied once again most likely. Eventually it will appear that the only way to dam the stream would be to build a dam from mountain to mountain, though it must be a thousand miles across to accomplish the purpose. In human affairs, such a constriction of the energies of a people is called totalitarianism, and it is this toward which government regulation and restraint tends.

Government regulation fails in the attainment of its purported object—often produces the opposite result—because of the nature of government, the nature of man, and the nature of economy. The nature of government is, or should be, very clear. It is that body, or those bodies, charged with the exclusive authority to employ *force* in a given jurisdiction. Force may be employed in two ways upon people. It may be used in support of *prohibitions* against certain kinds of actions. For example, murder may be prohibited, and force may be used to apprehend murderers or those caught in the act of attempting it, to hold them in jail, to bring them to trial, and to mete out punishment to those convicted. Or, force can be used to *induce* people to act in ways contrary to those to which they are bent. For example, force may be used on railroads to compel them to keep open stations which they would otherwise have closed.

A Proper Role for Government

A rather conclusive case can be made that governments can and ought to prohibit certain kinds of actions and punish offenders, a case as conclusive as any is likely to be in social matters. That is, an exceedingly strong case can be made that a body charged with the power to do so is necessary to the protection of life, liberty, and property and with the settlement of disputes which arise among men. A similar case can be made that the government so charged must have the power to compel the necessary support from those under its jurisdiction for the performance of its tasks. That is, government may collect taxes and may even compel peaceful men to take up arms to aid in the performance of these legitimate functions. (Of course, a government may be constitutionally limited as to how it goes about these things.)

No such conclusive case can be made for the use of government power to induce certain behavior in economic matters. On the contrary, men have quite sufficient inducement in the very nature of things to behave economically. Economy has to do with the frugal use of the elements of production—land, labor, and capital—to provide the goods and services most wanted. Everyman is inclined to do it this way. He is inclined to do as little work as possible to get the job done in the manner desired, to spend as little as he can to attain the quantity and quality of goods and services sought, and to use as little of his natural resources as will suffice. Indeed, he is inclined to use most frugally whichever of these are scarcest and to use most prodigally those which are in greatest supply. It is in his interest so to do.

Force is superfluous so far as it might be used to compel men to do what they would tend to do anyway by interest and inclination. It would not only be superfluous; it would be positively wasteful, for all the costs to provide the force would be above and beyond those necessary to get the job done.

Of course, governments do not employ force to get men to act in accord with their interests and inclinations. Government intervention into economy is an employment of force to induce men to do what would otherwise be contrary to their interests and inclinations. Even a superficial look at interventionist policies shows that this is their character. Governments intervene to induce companies to deal with labor unions, to induce men to join labor unions, to induce lenders to lend money at a lower rate than they could otherwise get, to induce employers to pay more than they would have to do to get employees, to induce companies to provide services which they would discontinue, to induce landlords to provide facilities at rates which are less profitable than they could get in the market, to induce men to charge more or less than it is in their interest to do.

Most of the government interventions in railroading have been of this character. Government intervened to compel railroads to deal with unions, to fix railroad rates below the market level, to compel the provision of unprofitable services, to induce railroads not to compete with one another in significant ways, to induce them to set up certain work rules, to induce them to share their facilities, and so on, through a story already told.

An Important Difference

Men do not cease to pursue their interests when government intervenes; they continue to do that as vigorously as ever. There is a very important difference, however. When men pursue their interests economically, they produce and provide the goods and services most wanted with the least use of resources. Government intervention changes both what appears to be most wanted and what appears to be the scarcest or most plentiful of resources. For example, when government offered a subsidy

Union Pacific Railroad Photo

Union Pacific Railroad Company's Domeliner, *The City of Portland,* in the Columbia River Gorge, Oregon.

for the production of cotton above the market price, it made cotton appear to be in greater demand than it was. When it restricted acreage to be planted to cotton simultaneously, it made land appear to be scarcer than it was. The result was that farmers, who were in a position to do so, devoted much more capital to the production of cotton, thus producing more cotton than could be sold at the supported price, hence surpluses of cotton.

The setting of a price or rate ceiling below the market price makes it appear that less of a good or service is wanted than actually is the case. This, of course, has happened with rail rates. One of the results has been the declining investment in the railroads. Another has been the reduction of services. Yet another was the meeting of the real demand for service by newer and other means of transport.

If wages are raised above the market price, this gives an appearance that labor is in shorter supply than, say, capital, though, in fact, there may be widespread unemployment. The tendency will be for labor to be replaced by machines, perhaps, at an accelerated pace, or, perhaps, by greater usage of natural resources.

To put the matter in broadest perspective, when government intervenes in one area, men shift their energies and attention to areas still left free or which may be relatively freer. For example, as the railroads were restricted and restrained, men turned more and more of their attention to the development of trucks, buses, automobiles, airplanes, and so forth. As the commercial uses of these have been increasingly regulated and restrained, the private transportation devices have been ever more extensively used.

Disintegrating Forces in Society

There are impacts to intervention which go beyond just the economic effects, though these are often devastating enough. Over the last several decades intervention in the economy has been growing and spreading. Government has turned more and more from its protective and prohibitive role toward a role as inducer and regulator. Laws for the protection of life, liberty, and property are still on the books in many instances, of course. The police still apprehend violators on numerous occasions. Juries still try and, as the case may be, convict those charged with such offenses. Beyond this point, however, the use of force to protect the citizenry has begun to break down. There is a widely expressed view that prisons are only for the rehabilitation of criminals, not for their punishment. There are even those who claim that punishment does not deter the commission of crimes (though some would restrict this view to crimes of passion). Once admit these premises, the criminal becomes an object of solicitude, and the use by government of force upon him becomes aggression. This is especially the case when it is also believed that the criminal is a victim of the society in which he has grown up.

For these and whatever other reasons there may be, many of the courts have taken to treating those charged with committing crimes with great solicitude. Their rights are ever more carefully protected in trials. Capital punishment has virtually disappeared. Probation after a short period of incarceration is commonplace, and suspended sentences are the order of the day.

This has occurred while government's use of force to intervene in economic matters has mounted. Statute books, state and national, are filled with minute and massive interventions ranging from the silly to the near catastrophic. The present writer has never encountered arguments to the effect that the threat of punishment will not induce people to pay their taxes, to obtain licenses, to refrain from forming trusts, to plant only the allotted acreage to crops, to obey the rulings of the Interstate Commerce Commission, to accept fiat money in payment of debts, to pay the minimum wage, to recognize and deal with the union certified by the National Labor Relations Board, and so on and on. Indeed, it is everywhere apparent that the threat of punishment must induce men to comply with a great maze of laws, many of which clearly run counter to their economic interest.

Soaring Crime Rates

In recent decades, crimes of aggression by individuals and groups have increased much faster than has the population. Such crimes as rape, aggravated assault, intimidation, robbery, and murder have become rampant. If trespass upon property were as strictly defined as it once was, the amount of violations would no doubt be much greater than it is. Intimidatory groups have frequently been permitted to terrorize selected peoples with impunity.

The connections between intervention in economic activities, on the one hand, and the tendency toward the breakdown of traditional law and order lie beneath the surface of things and are difficult to ferret out. One of them is the revolutionary thrust which gives impetus to the intervention. It is the desire to make over American society in an egalitarian fashion, and traditional protections of the individual must be broken down for the new society to emerge. Another connection is that the enforcement of the fantastic array of interventions overburdens government and leaves it weakened for its traditional tasks. Yet another is that the increasing force exercised by government has tended to disintegrate society so that social restraints on aggressive behavior are not as effective as formerly.

The impact of intervention, then, is disintegrating in its effects upon society, disruptive and diversive in men's efforts at economy, interferes with voluntary cooperation among individuals and groups, inhibits and redirects individual efforts, and is productive of confusion in industrial life. All too often, intervention produces the opposite of what would be wanted, produces an ineffective railroad system rather than a vital one, drives farmers from rural areas rather than making it possible for them to make a living, creates unemployment, takes away the value of men's savings, turns them away from serving one another to taking advantage of one another under the cover of governmental programs. Government intervention begets more government intervention. Just as a dam built across a river on an extensive plain will result in numerous rivulets which must in turn be dammed, so government intervention diverts men's energies into the remaining areas of freedom which must, in turn, be reduced in the vain hope that the earlier programs can be made to work. When an industry has finally been brought to heel in this fashion, it can no longer effectively perform its tasks. Government may then take over the industry directly or may subsidize it as an intermediate step to taking it over. Even now, this denouement is being acted out with the railroads.

Alternatives to Intervention

There is an alternative to intervention. To see it clearly we must redirect our sights. Government intervention proceeds by using force to induce men to act contrary to their interests. This, men will hardly do, though Draconian measures be applied against them. There is, however, a vast amount of energy to be found in people, energy which is only potential at its inception. A child at play shows how great is the energy available. Parents must have ever remarked that they wished they had only a fraction of the energy the child releases. The child runs first to this and then to that, whoops and hollers, invents some game which fascinates him for a moment, becomes bored quickly and turns to some other diversion. This is human energy in its raw state, giving the appearance of being bountiful because it is undisciplined and unrestrained.

The energy potential in man is great for either destruction or construction. No other being on this planet has ever shown the adeptness for destruction that men can do when they put their minds to it. They can burn whole cities, destroy crops, rape, pillage, kill, and lay waste. When they are bent upon construction they can devise and build such works of beauty and utility as no other creature could even imagine. They can build, heal, transport, provide food and raiment, manufacture, compute, educate, and use their brains and hands in thousands of ways wondrous to behold. Or, they can be so restricted and restrained by force that they neither destroy nor build with any will. Whole populations can be so enslaved or enserfed that their works do not live after them and their lives are little above brute level. Each of these potentialities of man has been fulfilled many times in the brief span of 4,000 years or so of recorded history.

The Constructive Use of Human Energy

Two things are necessary for the vast energy potential in men to be applied constructively. One is for the energy to be released. The other is for it to be disciplined so that it can be effectively applied. There is a major clue to the release of energy in the child at play. The child is following his own bent; he is *interested* in what he is doing, or, what he is doing interests him. To change this with a young child, it is necessary only to assign him to some task which he would call work. He will become tired almost at once. The abundant energy which he was just displaying will quickly disappear. He is no longer interested in what he is doing. Men are like that, too, though "interest" has become something much more extensive and comprehensive than it was for a child. Interest is not simply what gives him immediate pleasure. He has learned to defer immediate gratification for expected future gratifications. He works because it is in his interest to do so. He is interested not only in himself but in his wife, his children, perchance his parents, future grandchildren and a broader community which aids and protects him. He is interested in his rights and his possessions—his lands, houses, vehicles, and a hundred and one things which he owns or desires. His energies are readily released in defense of and in pursuit of a multitude of interests.

To release the energies of a man it is necessary to secure to him the fruits of his labor and the protection of his possessions. He will not willingly act against his interests, nor can he be readily induced to do so. Government intervention does, however, lead him to dissipate great quantities of energy to protect and advance his interests. Virtually all of this is so much waste. Americans today waste vast quantities of energy either in complying with government restrictions or finding ways to evade them. Not only that, but some of the regulations positively inhibit the employment of energy.

Discipline and its social corollary, organization, are essential to the constructive employment of energy. The broadened conception of his interests may lead a man to submit himself to discipline. A child may be trained to discipline and direct his energies. So may other social organizations. Great constructive activities frequently require that men cooperate with one another. This they find ways to do if they are restrained from injuring one another and are left free to pursue their own interests.

Much of the trouble in America today, as well as in much of the rest of the world, is that many organizations are arrayed against one another and some are deeply divided from within so that rather than facilitating constructive activities they are inhibiting them and dissipating energy in contests. Labor unions pit employees against employers. As American affairs have become more and more politicalized much of the energy of many organizations is devoted to gaining favors for the members, favors of wealth taken from the general populace by taxation. Both force and the possibilities of gaining such favors must be denied to organizations before they devote themselves to constructive activities once again.

The alternative to government intervention, then, is individual liberty. It is the release of the vast energies which men contain to constructive purposes. There is much that serves to help discipline man, but an invaluable support of self-discipline is the facility it gives him when he is able to pursue his interest. There are people today who would like to see passenger trains serving Americans at large once again. Some of these people believe that the way to achieve this end is to have government intervene. Yet intervention contains and diverts the energies of a people. It provides passenger trains at the expense of giving up other uses which people might prefer for their money. If there is a market sufficiently large to warrant passenger trains in America, it is most likely that railroads would provide them if the energies of their personnel were freed from the present confining restraints. If rate control were removed and investors could see clearly once again what was in demand, they would release funds in that direction. So it would be for a great range of goods and services which commercial establishments can hardly provide because of the restraints upon them.

Government intervention dams up and diverts the energies of the people; freedom releases them to constructive purposes.

Index

Prepared by Vernelia A. Crawford

The letter "n" following a number indicates a footnote.

U

W